PROVOCATIVE
FAITH

PROVOCATIVE
FAITH

walking away from ordinary

Matthew Paul Turner

Revell
Grand Rapids, Michigan

Published by Fleming H. Revell
a division of Baker Publishing Group
P.O. Box 6287, Grand Rapids, MI 49516-6287

Printed in the United States of America

Library of Congress Cataloging-in-Publication Data
Turner, Matthew Paul, 1973-
   Provocative faith : walking away from ordinary / Matthew Paul Turner.
     p.   cm.
   ISBN 0-8007-3092-5
   1. Christian life. I. Title.
   BV4501.3.T86 2005
   248.4—dc22   2005012674

For Daniel Eagan and Lisa Tedder,
who walked alongside of me out of the ordinary.

In memory of
Brian Bowdren—
a man of great faith and wisdom.

****

I tell you the truth,
if you have faith as small as a mustard seed,
you can say to this mountain,
"Move from here to there" and it will move.
Nothing will be impossible for you.

Matthew 17:20 NIV

contents

foreword

I met Matthew at an industry luncheon during Gospel Music week in Nashville a few years back. We instantly connected. His sincere interest in my "new" career in the Christian music industry was refreshing and down-to-earth.

Matthew is honest about the kind of music he likes. When he says he likes a song, I know he actually likes it. And when he doesn't, I know that too. It's Matthew's honesty that makes his writing so interesting for me. Even if you don't always agree with what he says, you can usually identify a familiar thread in what he writes that either you or someone you know has experienced.

Over the past few years, I've had a bird's-eye view of Matthew experiencing Jesus. Like the journey he so honestly portrays in *Provocative Faith*, he has walked through the good and the bad of life only to come out on the other side strengthened, though sometimes weary, but always ready to try again. And that's what I can identify with—the wrestling with God. Like Matthew, I always lose the wrestling match, but I always end stronger. Isn't that what the Christian life is like for all of us? Sometimes we're quick to learn the lessons Jesus is trying to teach us. But other times we get lost in the battle, hoping that somehow by fighting God he will eventually back down. Yet that's not how God works.

Most of the book simply tells us what Matthew has learned from God on his journey. I like this part because it's exactly how I experience God too. The God we serve is always faithful to reveal himself through our circumstances. Whether what we experience is good or bad or tragic, Jesus always intervenes on our behalf to teach us about our desperate *need* for him.

A month before my first album released, I visited Matthew at his home in Northern Virginia. During that time, he and I talked at length about our spiritual journeys. He shared with me the pain he'd experienced from the years of legalism he'd endured. I opened up and talked about how my faith in Christ had changed due to the loss of my first wife, Melissa, to cancer. In the quiet of a dark room, Matthew and I got facedown on the floor and prayed for each other. For nearly an hour, we confessed our sin, interceded on each other's behalf, and proclaimed the mercy and truth of Christ. That event represents for me exactly what he is trying to express when he uses the term *provocative*. Because that night we were no doubt convening with the Holy Spirit, and if that's not provocative, I don't know what is.

Jeremy Camp
recording artist

acknowledgments

Thank you, Jessica, for loving me beyond my imagination. Marrying you is the best thing I have ever done. God never ceases to amaze me through you, baby. Thank you to my wonderful family for your overwhelming investment. Each one of you has given me something I hold on to dearly. I am eternally indebted to your love and grace. Thank you to all of my friends (new and old) who have taught me so much about living provocatively. Thank you to each individual who allowed me to utilize his or her story so I could share mine. Thank you, Valerie Summers, for believing in my work. Thank you, Stephen, Janella, and everyone else at Twentys. I look forward to seeing where this ride goes! Jennifer Leep at Revell Books, this dream began with you taking a chance on me; I owe you my gratitude. I also want to thank Twila Bennett, Aaron Carriere, Cheryl Van Andel, Trish Konieczny, and Paul Brinkerhoff at Revell Books. Thank you, Jesus, for making my faith in you provocative.

introduction

provocative faith

Because we know that this extraordinary day is just ahead,
we pray for you all the time—pray that our God will make
you fit for what he's called you to be.

2 Thessalonians 1:11

Two years ago, I met Henry, an eighty-something-year-
old man with a big, infectious smile. Our running into
each other was one of those chance meetings at an airport.
(I'm notorious for meeting interesting people at airports;
I have a habit of talking to anyone.) Henry and I were
on the same flight from Nashville to Baltimore—but as it
turned out, we weren't flying anywhere at the moment.
The airline attendant made an announcement that the
plane was having engine trouble, so we were forced to wait
in the crowded gate area until further notice. Henry had
already caught my eye. He was hard to miss dressed in a
bright yellow T-shirt that proudly stated his opinion on

an upcoming political election. I watched Henry get out
of the long line. He smiled kindly at the gate attendant,
slowly picked up his old-fashioned, hard, black suitcase,
and sat down one chair over from me. Henry was a true
Southerner, complete with a blue and white paisley hand-
kerchief protruding out of his front pocket. He was on his
way to the D.C. area to visit his daughter and son-in-law
and their new baby girl, Samantha.

Before long Henry and I were talking about the weather,
complaining about the plane delay, and debating about
the upcoming NCAA basketball tournament. Talking with
Henry made the wait a lot easier. His voice was soothing,
and his smile would have lit up a funeral home if given
the chance. Henry's only downfall was being a fan of the
University of North Carolina Tarheels. (I'm a fan of their
rival Duke University.) But even before Henry opened his
mouth, I already knew that he was a man of faith. Isn't it
funny how you can sometimes tell?

Soon Henry and I were conversing about Jesus's influence on our lives. Henry had once served as a Methodist
minister of a small-town church about thirty miles north-
east of Nashville. He retired from full-time ministry when
he was seventy-five. "Although," he added with a grin,
"the Lord's work is never something you really retire from.
You just stop getting paid for it."

He went on to tell me a small part of his story. For
thirty minutes or so, he talked about his duties during the
Second World War, the loss of his beloved Katherine ten
years before, and where he was when Kennedy got shot
and on September 11. The old man shared his favorite
moments as a minister preaching for a small community

church and talked enthusiastically about the joy he finds in each of his seven grandbabies. He was a gentle old soul, with an exuberant sense of humor and a simple way with words.

"Young man," said Henry at one point, looking straight into my eyes, "I believe an individual finds fulfillment when he builds his faith around loving Jesus with all of his heart, cherishes his family, and forgives his friends. That's what Daddy always told me. He'd also say, 'Do right, Henry; do right until the stars fall.' I've tried to live by that motto. In everything I've pursued, I've tried to pursue what was good and right. And always do my best. But most importantly, I worked at getting to know Jesus. Too many people today do not take the time to really get to know their Savior, their faith . . . It's sad, really."

There was a simple wisdom in Henry's words that made me want to spend the entire evening with him. Even in our short conversation, he was already giving me advice about life. I liked his blunt spirit. Too often I don't have the guts to "shoot straight" with people. Henry had strong convictions, and he wasn't afraid to communicate them. He wasn't afraid to speak into someone else's life. Sure, he wasn't sharing anything that I hadn't heard a thousand times before. But when he said those familiar words, they had life—stories and wrinkles to back them up. And his passion resonated with me. I left that conversation and walked onto a very late flight to Baltimore's BWI Airport, feeling inspired to be something more than a spectator in this life of faith.

Over the years, I've spoken to many individuals about their relationship with God. And I've noticed that people often act funny when they start talking about their faith. Conversations about God invoke different emotions in different people. Some of us get too serious. Some of us get misty-eyed and start crying like babies. Others are nonchalant in talking about their religious beliefs. A few of us are careless and whimsical. I know some people who get loud, obnoxious, and hyper when they talk about all things spiritual. Others stay reserved and focused. But despite all the different attitudes, perspectives, and personalities regarding faith in Jesus Christ, I have found that most of us desire similar things.

Most of us want our spiritual life to have electricity and excitement, comfort and warmth, devotion and peace. But that's not all. We want the answers to all of the hard spiritual questions. We want to be certain of God's will and his ultimate plans for us. We want to feel centered and healthy and truly understand what it means to be a lover of our Savior Jesus. And once in a while, we want to see a miracle or two that inspire us to keep on the straight and narrow. We don't ask for a burning bush or the healing of a blind man; we'd be content with something much less extravagant. We just need a little something that will give us a few more questions to ponder. But most importantly, we want to see the presence of Jesus shining brightly through us—often.

We want to be moved by our faith. And we want our faith to motivate us to respond with good deeds and tangible love toward others. Scratch beneath the surface of even those Christians who seem complacent or comfortable or stuffy, and you'll almost always find an individual who longs for so much more than what the church or religiosity stands for or what preachers talk about on Sunday mornings.

Sadly, though, too few Christians can claim to have ever experienced a profound spiritual encounter with the God of the universe. The average follower of God lets obstacles get in the way of wholeheartedly embracing a complete faith in Jesus. We hesitate to be ourselves in our relationship with Jesus. We live our Christian lives vicariously through preachers, teachers, praise and worship leaders, and Bible study gurus. We're afraid to ask questions. We're scared to have doubts. We live with an overwhelming amount of guilt. And despite our disappointing circumstances and our disheartening lack of personal experience, we feel obligated to claim exuberantly that *"yes, we are alive in Christ."* Which means these words are oftentimes simply lip service. Being *alive* in Christ means living a life of faith in him—not in the guilt, fear, and the questions we're afraid to ask. Surely faith in Christ encompasses our questions, our fears, and our doubts, as well as our convictions, freedoms, and personalities.

Madeleine L'Engle once said, "Those who believe they believe in God but without passion in the heart, without anguish of mind, without uncertainty, without doubt, and even at times without despair, believe only in the idea of God, and not in God Himself." I believe Ms. L'Engle lists the very things that describe someone who is fully alive: passion and anguish, uncertainty, doubt, and sometimes even despair.

God wants us to be truly alive—in every meaning of the word. He made us to be intimate, passionate, creative, thinking creatures for a reason. But many of us, instead of using these characteristics to pursue our relationship with God, end up presenting him with leftovers, the boring stuff, the "*same ole same ole.*" Or—worse still—we regurgitate someone else's affections, hoping they will somehow ring true. What Jesus hears from us is all too often just the same rhetoric he's heard a million times before from a million other people. Many times it's not really our fault; we're just repeating what we've been taught to say to God. I don't necessarily think God is angered by such offerings, but I do think he often finds more praise, worship, and glory in the birds, rocks, and trees than he finds in his followers. I don't half blame him—I've often found birds to be more satisfying companions than some Christians too.

Several years ago, I was driving home from work on a Wednesday evening. The sky was lit up with a hundred different colors as the sun began to say good-bye for the evening. And there was an unexplainable stillness in my soul that I found hard to ignore. God was trying to speak. It always gets strangely still when God is trying to speak to me. So I turned off the radio and began to listen, and he gently started to move my thoughts.

He reminded me of the story of Moses standing before a very settled Red Sea. I thought about how nervous Moses must have been as he anticipated the power of God to reveal itself. And I wondered if Moses had thought to himself, *God, are you there?* But then at that moment, as the day was on the verge of giving in to the night, God said to me, "Moses's faith in *my* strength wasn't perfect, but I used it to do great things. I desire to use you too." That moment was a split-second nudge on my heart that

18

seemed to last forever. It wasn't a visible sign like the Red Sea parting, but it was a moment that reminded me of God's abiding hold on my life and his expectation of my faith in him.

Jesus's expectation of me is to be a human fully in love with him. But I can't love fully until my entire self is fully engaged in the process. I have learned in my life of faith that when I'm not truly real with my Father, when I'm not diving completely into what he has for me, I miss out on truly knowing him—knowing his vast mercies, his fanatical love, and his breathtaking miracles. I miss out on living a complete faith—not a perfect faith, but complete.

Consider the men and women of faith in Old Testament Scripture. Each of these godly individuals had a unique relationship with God. David was an emotional man whose love for God embodied his whole being. David used his emotion to worship God freely. He danced. He sinned. He conquered. I don't believe anyone can question the fact that David had an intimate relationship with the Father.

Daniel was consistent and fervent in his pursuit of God. His faith was practical and enduring. Some might consider Daniel's faith to be a bit rough around the edges, but he pursued God in a way that came naturally to him, and God was pleased.

Ruth was humble and meek, yet brave. Her faith was simple. Throughout her story, we read about a young woman who matured from a faith that simply followed others' actions into a personal faith of passion and grace.

The faith of Ruth, Daniel, and David manifested itself in completely different ways, but God received glory in watching *each* of them pursue him with every part of their being. They had questions, doubts, fears, frustrations, and disappointments, and still their faith in a powerful God was real.

Consider Jesus's quest to invite the simpleminded to follow him during his ministry here on earth. Many of the circumstances we read about in the Gospels find Jesus looking for simplicity of faith. Jesus praised the woman who dropped her twopence into the offering basket because she had faith enough to give all she owned. Jesus embraced children because their love was not superficial and masked—they put all of their being into loving him. And as frustrating as Peter was at times, Jesus saw something in Peter that moved him. Peter had the bravery to blindly jump into faith. Sure, he looked ridiculous at times, and he failed miserably, but he truly wanted to experience a living Christ. Jesus liked that.

I know many people who just seem to spiritually get it. They take Jesus at his word and live life with a faith that embodies everything they are. Mistakes don't stop them. Doubt is a part of life that they can anticipate and work through gracefully. It almost feels like the energy of Christ just surrounds these individuals. They're alive. They listen, love, and live with an abandonment that's hard to comprehend.

Have you ever met someone like that—the kind of man or woman whose very actions you want to emulate? I've known quite a few such people. And I must admit that I've often been envious of them. They just seem to know Jesus intimately. There's no perfect definition for such a person. Their faith is not fake, pretentious, or gaudy; it's just visible and contagious and exciting. And you want some of it. I did too.

A couple of years ago, Jesus woke me up. And began a journey with a simple quest. It was my personal goal to discover the secret of an individual faith in God. This book is a chronicle of that journey—a journey of all God has taught me about faith and being alive in him. I share it because I hope it makes you contemplate your own faith. Are you where you want to be spiritually? My hope is that this book inspires you to begin your own journey. Don't imitate my journey. Simply use these chapters to help you discover or rediscover the truths that Jesus wants all of us to know. No doubt a life of faith should be centered, stimulating, controversial, challenging, powerful, miraculous, vulnerable, frustrating, and fearful—in a word, provocative.

Enjoy,
Matthew Paul Turner
matthew@matthewpaulturner.com

a prologue

the road

All of us have different jumping-off points; this story is mine.

Eight years ago, at the age of twenty-four, I was standing in what many Christians consider the perfect worship position. My hands were raised high and spread apart. My eyes were closed tightly. My facial expression hung somewhere between constipation and complete surrender. My feet were shoulder-width apart, and my legs were slightly bent at the knees. I was singing the words of "Lord, I Lift Your Name on High" with intensity and charisma and perhaps just a little bit of snobbery for a subtle "I'm religious" effect. At the time, I was absolutely certain that most worship pastors would have been quite impressed with my devotion to worshiping my Lord and Savior Jesus Christ. I was playing the part very well.

But every once in a while during the music, my ADD would get the best of me, and I would look around the large room and covertly observe others in the church as they stood in an array of various worship positions. A lovely, large black lady with big braids in her hair danced in the aisle on the other side of the auditorium. I watched her with pleasure, but I secretly envied her ability to praise God with such freedom of expression. There was a blonde girl next to me who jarringly hit my elbows every time she lifted her hands. Tears ran down the left side of her cheek, and she was murmuring something quietly to herself. I tried to eavesdrop, but I couldn't understand what she was saying. So my eyes scurried over to a tall, skinny, and homely college student whose twistingly expressive face made him look as though his insides were about to come out of him. He made my own "constipation and surrender" worship expression seem rather tame.

At that moment, it looked as if the entire congregation were lost in the tranquility of a "God moment." "Thank you, Jesus," one man screamed at the top of his lungs.

"Lord God, we want to hear from you this morning," cried another.

I looked over at the second "yeller," but one of the deacons caught me looking around, so I immediately closed my eyes and started singing again.

Then suddenly, the final song ended. The praise and worship leader said a prayer. People stretched. One older gentleman yawned. The big, black lady stopped dancing. My neighbor stopped crying *and* concluded her murmuring. The college kid looked *relaxed* again. It felt like someone had just gotten on the loudspeaker and cried, "Ladies and gentlemen, the Spirit of the living God has just left the building." Because no doubt as quickly as he had arrived, he was out.

Within moments of God's quick exit, a bunch of my friends and I were busy saying hello, hugging each other, commenting on how awesome today's worship service made us feel, and making plans to head to T.G.I. Friday's for a quick after-church get-together. In the midst of discussing our lunch plans, I offered my take of "Gosh, that last song was amazing—I had Jesus-bumps all over me." My friends all agreed.

We then spent the lunchtime hour discussing the sermon, critiquing the music, commenting on the soloist's dress, and sharing with each other what we had taken away from the service.

This routine was a weekly occurrence for me. Sunday mornings would come and go without a hitch. Every week I'd show up a few minutes before the service would begin and save a couple of seats for friends before the praise and worship music started. The presence of God usually showed up at exactly the same time every Sunday morning—10:02—just about two minutes into the first song. I watched him fall first on those who were standing on the stage and in the front rows. From there he would quickly work his way around the congregation. He stayed for exactly one hour and fifteen minutes, and then he'd leave, always right on schedule. Although, looking back, I'm inclined to think he sometimes went to the bathroom about twelve minutes into the pastor's sermon.

To be honest with you, I was never so sure that the Holy Spirit really was descending on us every Sunday morning. But I was probably the only one who thought this, because every one of my friends was thoroughly convinced that on Sunday morning, church was the only place to be if you had any plans of convening with the Holy Spirit. And maybe he *was* there. The truth is by that time in my life, I was so jaded with the act I was putting on that I probably would have found reason to criticize Jesus if he had shown up in flesh and bone on Sunday morning.

As I look back on that time in my life, I realize that although I regularly worshiped, read my Bible, taught a children's Sunday school class, sang in the choir, and did almost all the other good things I thought a twenty-something Christian should do, a part of me was spiritually dying. I felt like my faith had been beaten up, bruised, and left for dead in a pew somewhere in Maryland. I was tired of playing church. I was sick of the rhetoric. I wanted more out of my faith.

Like many of you reading this book, I was raised in church. My backside resided in a pew every Sunday morning, Sunday night, and Wednesday night. When I was a kid, I actually thought we were in church more often than we were at home.

My parents loved Jesus, and they worked hard to raise my three sisters and me in a godly home. As a four-year-old boy, seeing what Dad and Mom had found in Jesus made me want to get up out of my chair and walk down the aisle to get "saved." And although the beginning of my road of faith was substantially paved with Bible stories, vacation Bible school, and more, I realized sooner rather than later that building one's entire faith around the church was foolishness. But that's what I was taught to do.

By the time I was in my midtwenties, my faith in Jesus Christ had become more of a habit than a life-altering existence. My Christian background had been filled with Bible thumping of gargantuan proportions. I had felt the grip of legalism wrap its tentacles around my heart, and it squeezed the life right out of me. The more I moved and shifted, the stronger the grip became. And even after God began to free me from that graceless life, past memories of ridiculous church screwups and stupid pulpit proclamations kept me from experiencing Jesus—his freedom, peace, justice, and mercy. So instead of running from legalism into the freeing arms of Jesus, I ran headfirst toward a life consumed with criticism, sarcasm, and bitterness.

In the middle of that wrestling match with God, I believed that I had seen, experienced, and passed judgment on everything Christian culture had to offer. I eventually became numb to the spiritual "stuff" that swirled around me. I couldn't see the truth of Jesus Christ to save my life, and in fact, I had become even resistant to it. Anything remotely resembling my past spiritual experiences left me feeling nauseated.

However, I truly wanted to experience Jesus. At times, I even thought I was doing so. But I realize now that my heart was held hostage by the tainted faith of my past. If Jesus would have pinched me, I doubt I would have *really* felt it. I would have known he had just pinched me, I would have been able to see the red and white mark his two-fingered squeeze had left behind, but my heart would still have been careless toward him. I had developed a form of complacency toward everything "Christian," and a part of me was already beginning to decay.

On the outside, I don't believe most people noticed what was going on in me. I had learned from my childhood days, which I spent impressing deacons and wowing pastors, how to hide what was going on inside my head. It was easy. A forced smile, a contemplative glance, or a firm and honest handshake always impressed them.

So I smiled on the outside, and I kept the inside—rebellion, lust, fear, complacency, bitterness—locked up for fear of its consequences. But wrapped up inside me, those things were suffocating my soul. I was yielding to the pressure of church rhetoric, mean-spirited Christians, and bad theology—not to mention my own bouts with personal sin.

I never questioned my need for a personal relationship with Jesus; all along, I knew I *needed* him. But instead of pursuing him and leaving everything else behind, I tried to take on the religious establishment. I pretended it was religion, not God, I had a problem with. But no matter where I aimed my frustrations, my bitterness toward all things churched was beginning to take root.

I tried to keep my composure, but I had so many questions running through my head that eventually some of them began reaching for the surface. I tried to keep from asking too many questions out loud, because whenever I did, someone would hand me a Christian book by Ravi Zacharias or Philip Yancey. Heck, when people asked *me* hard spiritual questions, I usually handed them a book by Ravi or Phil. And nothing against these two fine authors, but truthfully, I had become very tired of reading Christian books by authors who many Christians had told me would have all the answers. I was sick of reading chapter after chapter filled with terms like *transforming, rediscovering*, and *grace-filled*. It seemed like Christian books always made life seem too perfect and pretty. My spiritual life was far from perfect and pretty. To someone like me who felt very bruised by the evangelical system, perfect and pretty didn't really sound all that great.

When I reached that point in my life, I realized that bitterness had taken hold of my spiritual life so much that I couldn't enjoy truth. I was so caught up in criticizing and judging the world around me that I missed out on the simple words of Jesus. Sure, I had friends who reminded me that God was with me. But I didn't hear them. I couldn't hear them. I felt like my faith journey was at a dead end.

That dead end, though lonely and hard, ended up being a beautiful place for me. Finally, I couldn't keep running away. Unless I wanted to beat my head up against the brick wall that stood in front of me (and I resisted the temptation to do that), I could do no more harm to my spiritual self. In my mind, I had run out of good options—you know, a dead end.

King David often suspected he was at a dead end. In Psalm 22:1–2 David says, "God, God . . . my God! Why did you dump me miles from nowhere? Doubled up with pain, I call to God all the day long. No answer. Nothing. I keep at it all night, tossing and turning." There are times in his writing when you sense David was depressed, worried, and overcome with grief. The first few verses of Psalm 35 say, "Harass these hecklers, GOD, punch these bullies in the nose. Grab a weapon, anything at hand; stand up for me! Get ready to throw the spear, aim the javelin, at the people who are out to get me. Reassure me; let me hear you say, 'I'll save you'" (vv. 1–3).

I looked in the mirror one day not too long ago and realized I was a complete mess. I honestly began to laugh out loud at the thoughts I was processing and at my obviously flawed perspective on faith. Although much of what I thought wasn't at all funny, I couldn't help but laugh at my wandering journey and the lopsided burden I had been carrying with me.

And that day, standing in front of the mirror, I began a new journey toward knowing Jesus. I'm still on that journey. It's a hard path full of frustrations and fears. But it's also an exciting and invigorating road.

The chapters that follow are truths I have learned about living a full, life-filled, provocative faith. I believe these truths will help anyone desiring to truly know Jesus fully and completely.

1

humans weren't meant to live in cages

October 22, 1998, was a whirlwind of a day. It was on that Sunday evening when my personal relationship with Jesus hit a breaking point. I wasn't at a church service or a revival or a music concert. I was home alone, sinning.

On that evening, I had come to Jesus with yet another confession. I think I must have been known in heaven for my many confessions. I made a habit of confessing my sin. Nearly every time I fell short of God's glory—which was often—I'd offer Jesus my apology. This particular time, I was apologizing for my regular once-every-couple-of-months bout with sexual gratification through the beautiful convenience of online pornography.

Locked away in my bedroom, I had spent the better half of that Sunday afternoon diving headfirst into my own little world of sexual images. I invested three *glorious* hours into high-speed downloadable ecstasy. I wasn't addicted to porn—at least, *I* didn't think so—but I did have a haphazardly scheduled, few-times-a-year habit. It was my little secret. It was one of many sinful habits on a list that included pride, low self-esteem, selfishness, and anger, all of which I would often try to kick cold turkey, to no avail.

My regular stint with sin always included a "fall flat on my face before God" declaration of repentance. It was always a heartfelt, beautifully executed climaxing dismount. I had perfected the art of confessing. And this particular confession was no different. My guilt-induced Jesus-whimpering began shortly after my cyber-escapade ended. "Jesus, I am *so* sorry. If you forgive me one more time, I will never let this happen again" was my usual plea bargain. But I meant what I said. I truly thought it would never happen again. I hated sinning—not necessarily because of the act itself—but because of the way it made me feel afterward: *gross and unworthy—right up there with child molesters and rapists and abortionists.* One time the guilt from sin hit me so hard that I literally became nauseated and ended up vomiting in the office toilet.

God had been enduring my repulsive apology routine for years: I'd sin, I'd feel guilty; I'd fall on my face and ask for forgiveness, and *bam*—I'd be forgiven. It worked this way every single time. In my mind, there wasn't any chance God wouldn't accept me back into his ever-loving arms. I knew that freedom and grace were a part of his character, and I made a habit of taking advantage of that.

Every single time I went to God and asked for his forgiveness, I had *always* been taken back into his arms rather quickly. Almost instantly, after saying a few quick words, I would feel comfort again. I foolishly assumed that it was his responsibility to forgive me and make me feel better. Let's face it—he's the God of grace and mercy, right? A waiting period with God is not common; it was my experience that he was quick, to the point, and *always* there.

For me, Jesus was my personal "God ATM." Every time I needed acceptance or mercy or love or grace or freedom, I would just go to the ATM and get a withdrawal. And *that* day was no different. Even though I had spent the better part of an afternoon giving in to the temptation of sin, I had no doubt that I would soon feel the warmth of his graceful presence just like many times before; he always listened to me with his merciful ear. *Always!*

However on *that* day, it was a very different story. On *that* day, God wasn't listening to my negotiating. It seemed my prayers weren't reaching heaven. I said them over and over again, but I still failed to feel at peace with my situation.

The ATM seemed to be out of order—or maybe out of funds. There were no gracious arms hugging me and patting me on the back such as I had always experienced before. No one was telling me, "It's going to be okay, Matthew." Instead of comfort, hope, and forgiveness, I felt very alone, abandoned, and caged—and I passionately hated that feeling.

My first thought was that perhaps God hadn't heard me ask him for forgiveness the first time. So I begged some more, and this time, I said it louder—even trying to make it seem more meaningful than before. "God, I am *so sorry* for what I've been doing. *Please don't take your blessings away from me. Please forgive me.* I want to feel better. I need *you.*"

Although I was rather impressed with those words and my perfect delivery style, still there was no word from Jesus. He wasn't making any effort to make me feel better. At that point, a million thoughts started running through my head. *This is it,* I realized. *He's finally fed up with my disgusting shenanigans, and he's going to unveil me as the foolish bastard that I am.* And still he was silent. He had never been silent with me before. I didn't know what to do. I hate silence. It's one thing when someone is just quiet because there's nothing to talk about, but when someone is silent *on purpose* because they no longer want to partake in a conversation with you—that's a whole other story. But I believe now that we can all learn from those uncomfortable moments when God is silent.

Consider the moments in biblical history when God was silent toward his people for a long period of time. Remember Joseph and his run-in with Potipher's wife? She made a sexual advance toward him; he refused her advance—even ran out of the bedroom. The woman became embarrassed and irritated with Joseph, so she told her husband that Joseph had tried to force himself on *her.* Poor Joseph ended up spending fourteen years in prison for a crime he never committed. And God remained silent in Joseph's situation. Only a few times did Joseph get a glimpse of hope that he would one day be free. But for the better part of fourteen excruciating years, God seemed to be absent in Joseph's life. When God is silent, it's easy to get frustrated and angry over his apparent lack of interest in what is going on in your particular life situation.

So when God seemed to ignore my cry for forgiveness, I did what came naturally to me (something that comes naturally to all of us, I guess): I went back to the comfort of my sin. Instead of hating my sin, instead of despising the thing that was keeping me from living my life freely, I set up house in a cage of my own desires, where I was my own god and made my own rules—where I could get what I wanted. I began learning how to survive (and even enjoy) the confines of my tainted environment. I decided to get comfortable in my surroundings, thinking to myself, *Well, if God isn't going to help me out, I'll help myself out.* So I put all of my time, energy, and emotion into pleasing me. And that's what I did. And it felt good for a while—*really* good.

Humans are certainly prone to living in cages. Cages are often comfortable, plush surroundings that offer the illusion of freedom. Oh, people's cages look different, feel different, and can consist of many different things, but no matter how you dress a cage up, it's still a cage.

A cage is anything that keeps us from being completely free—from sin, mediocrity, religion, power, culture, and much more. Cages often keep us from pursuing the hopes and dreams Jesus has placed in our hearts. Cages lock us away inside familiarity or pleasure. Cages can make us unhappy, depressed, and self-consumed, but they can also make us feel invigorated and free. Many people are quick to equate their cages to sin, and often that's the case. But cages aren't limited to sin. Surprisingly, many humans find themselves caged by church, family, jobs, extracurricular activities, knowledge, friends, pop culture, philosophies, and thousands of other things—and certainly sin too.

The craftsmanship of an individual's cage depends greatly on the things he or she has been taught, accustomed to, or believes to be true. I have a dear friend who was taught during his childhood to fear anything remotely religious. When James came to know Jesus in 1999, it was through the unconventional means of his research for a college psychology paper on the impact of Christian ministries in urban communities. After seeing how the faith-based organizations influenced the lives of inner-city children, my friend became a believer in Jesus, but not in the church. James's cage was his inability to trust any organized religious practice. After two years of counseling, in 2001 James walked into his first community of faith and worshiped for the first time with other Christians. He says this of his experience: "My parents are atheists, and their influence on my thinking crippled my ability to be free. I had learned that *nothing* good comes from inside the walls of a church building. It wasn't until I decidedly moved against that teaching that I saw how deeply affected I was by what I considered to be true."

Jesus wasn't kidding when he said that truth will set you free (see John 8:32). Yet despite our quick habit to claim

Jesus has freed us from our sins, so many of us end up not fully understanding what that freedom truly means.

Most of us know that when we ask Jesus to come into our hearts (the salvation experience), we are instantly made new creatures in the eyes of God. In essence, Jesus puts his seal of approval on us, and we are made right and holy before God. Before we come to grips with the sacrifice of Christ, we are nothing more than condemned individuals destined for an eternity apart from God. But we have the assurance that when Jesus came into our lives, he made us free from future judgment. To break it down in nonspiritual terms, it's a makeover of sorts—and it's *extreme*.

This particular kind of freedom (the freedom from the punishment for our sin) is the beginning of faith. It's the jumping-off point. Without freedom from sin through the blood sacrifice of Christ, there is no faith journey. This is where a relationship with Christ begins. This is where Jesus wakes us up to his purpose for us—living a life of faith. Submitting yourself to what Christ did on the cross is the single most important decision you can make. (You probably already know that.) Because without Christ, it's futile to even try to get out of our cages.

But for me, even though I knew Jesus had freed me from my sin, my misunderstanding of freedom in Christ restrained me from truly experiencing the liberty that Jesus offers each of us. I think this is true for many people of faith. If we truly want to experience Jesus to the fullest and live extraordinarily, though, we must pursue *complete* freedom.

After we begin following Jesus, most of us join churches, begin reading faith-based books and devotionals, start pursuing Christian relationships, and invest ourselves into the "Christian" way of life. We pick up many "Christian" practices, beliefs, and ideals along the way. Our understanding of Scripture, evangelism, and Jesus is shaped by all the "Christian stuff." Over time, many of us become quite dependent upon our theology, doctrine, good deeds, and overall love of Christian things. Our church life begins to influence our politics, the people we hang out with, the way we handle family crisis, our view of sexuality and relationships, the jobs we choose to explore, our opinions about sin, and so much more. Sometimes these influences are built around the truth of the gospel, but often they are not. So often what influences our behavior is humanity's opinions of truth. These opinions often become the beginning framework for our future cages. In an effort to remain free, we read more books, go to different churches, and pursue more Christian relationships. This way of life becomes a vicious cycle that eats away at our faith and paralyzes our ability to keep focused on the journey.

Consequently, many of us end up lost in a great deal of spiritual confusion. Some of us run away from our faith, but most of us stay in hopes of one day coming to an understanding. We become confused about petty issues like whether it's right or wrong to drink alcohol or to kiss on a first date. We spend precious time debating such issues. We even write books on these topics. And even more frustrating than our indecisiveness about the right and wrong of basic human behavior is the sad fact that our cages inhibit our ability to share our faith. Our ability to be a witness is limited by the rules we've been subject to all our lives. Past mistakes like divorce, drug addiction, and unmarried sex become the foundations for guilt-ridden futures lived inside cages.

Too often we end up living caged lives for Jesus. Do you call that living? I don't.

A twenty-two-year-old African American woman named Ruthie once told me that she was having a difficult time being sexually intimate with her new husband. I'm not sure why, but this bothered me, so being somewhat blunt, I asked her why. She told me that as a child she had always been taught by her mother the importance of purity. "I can still hear Momma telling me not to let a man touch me," said Ruthie. "And now it's stuck with me. It's very difficult for me to just let go and be free with the man I love and am married to. I feel guilty trying to be *sexy* for him."

I know a little about what Ruthie is feeling. I grew up in a church that harped on purity as the be-all and end-all of truth. Instead of focusing on my motives or my heart condition, the Christian individuals I lived among were constantly watching to see if I was going to screw up. Some of them even seemed to hope I would. So instead of learning how to respect a woman, I learned how not to get caught. And that was a cage I had to be freed from—a cage that has caused me much pain and anxiety as an adult.

I've met some Christians who have blamed their struggle with homosexuality on the heavy-handed rhetoric of the church. Paul Thyme, a friend of mine from my college days, says his feelings toward the same sex began because the church was so adamant about men not being intimate with women. "Don't touch girls, don't sit too close, you better look the other way when a woman walks by—I remember it all," Paul told me in a phone conversation last year. "I didn't want to struggle, but if you take women completely out of a young man's life and replace them with circumstances like prepubescent boys taking showers together after a ballgame—some guys, even Christian guys, are going to have problems. At least, I did." Paul added that he feels he would have been able to be free from his cage much sooner had gay issues not been such a taboo topic among family, friends, and the church. Paul's cage wasn't so much the concept of being gay as it was his inability to discuss his situation openly. In secret, he battled guilt, hidden "friendships," and thoughts of suicide.

Ruthie and Paul weren't meant to live in these cages. Followers of Jesus are meant to live free. But in both instances, a graceless teaching from their past kept them locked up emotionally, mentally, and spiritually.

Some cages are simply based on false data.

I was seventeen years old when doctors told me that I needed back surgery to correct my scoliosis (a curvature of the spine)—a battle I had been fighting since I was four years old. I didn't want to have surgery, so I asked God to heal me. I remember sitting in front of the TV several weeks before my surgery date, listening to a televangelist tell me that if I truly believed God could heal me, I should lay one hand on the TV. I was skeptical of this approach, but I really wanted to be healed and had no doubt God could do it.

With faith, fear, and expectation all wrapped up in a tight knot within my gut, I placed my hand on the face of the television set. The preacher then proceeded to pray on my behalf for healing, and I guess on the behalf of others too. When he said "Amen," I firmly believed I was healed.

Although I didn't feel much different, I just knew that God had made my back straight. I took off my shirt, stood in front of the bathroom mirror, and convinced myself that my spine was straight. My heart was filled with hope and excitement.

A week later, I went in for my final checkup. I was certain that when the doctors looked at the X-ray, they would return with some miraculous news. I would then give God all the glory.

While I sat in one of the observation rooms at A. I. Dupont Children's Hospital in Wilmington, Delaware, the anticipation was killing me. Finally, the doctors returned.

"Well, Matthew, . . . " said the doctor.

This is it. God has healed me; I just know it. There isn't going to be any surgery.

". . . with your surgery being next week, we'll need you to come in tomorrow to begin giving blood."

What?!? You mean I still have to have the operation?

I was speechless, disappointed, and tearful, lost in my cage of misconstrued theology. It wasn't until many years later that I began to break free from petty theological idiosyncrasies such as this.

Whether it's codependency on someone or an unhealthy relationship with family or insecurities with image and sexuality, everyone's cages are different. Christians talk with such passion about freedom, yet many of us have no concept of what it means to be truly free.

Many times we are controlled and manipulated by bad doctrine. And the only remedy for bad doctrine is to hold on for dear life to what we know to be true—that there is no guilty verdict for those whom Jesus knows. We are intoxicated by the passions, disasters, and influences of culture instead of standing firm on the gospel's integrity and peace. We are overcome with the power to judge and be separate instead of humbly ignoring what exists to our right and left and keeping our hearts, minds, and actions on the gospel of Jesus Christ.

We settle for living within the restricted quarters of our own personal cages rather than forging ahead in freedom and confidence. Christians must stop building cages. We must passionately pursue freedom. It is freedom that must be set free if we want to see, feel, and experience the Spirit of a living God destroying our cages.

2

freedom is the beginning of faith

On October 23, the day after my fiasco with sin, God was still giving me the silent treatment. Gosh, I hate it when he gets quiet. So instead of me being silent, I did what many stupid Christians do—I retaliated. I said to God, "I'll show you what I'm really capable of." I took another hit of lust-filled satisfaction. This time, though, I needed more than just a three-hour session. I locked myself away in my room for the entire day and filled my heart and mind with junk meant to make me feel good.

At first, my plan worked like a charm—I completely forgot about the fact that God and I were not on speaking terms. As far as I was concerned, we both had retreated to our separate corners. And when you're desperate and angry, sin has a way of temporarily filling your emptiness.

However, by the end of the day, after I had immersed myself again into my own filth and was sitting alone in my own stench, I was ready for God and me to start talking. So I went banging on his door—*again*. I gave him the same spiel I'd always used. The "I'm-so-sorry-please-love-me-again" confessional that had always worked before. I was at a loss about why God wasn't speaking or moving or making me feel better like he had done so many times before. Why was he quiet?

The longer God was silent, the more self-consumed I became and the more comfortable my surroundings became. I tried to find solace and pity in my friends, but they didn't want to hear my whining. It almost seemed like God had given them the heads-up on our disagreement, and I was the only one left out of the loop.

I felt completely abandoned for four days. It seemed as though I was on an island and no one could get to me, and I could contact no one. I tried to make contact with God, but nothing was effective. I'd exhausted every method of God communication I knew, just short of putting a note in a bottle and throwing it out the window of my bedroom. I can see now that God had an unnervingly brilliant plan hidden up his sleeve.

God was about to teach me about real freedom—freedom you feel and don't just talk about.

After five days of utter silence, God finally opened his mouth. It wasn't his loud, booming voice. But it wasn't necessarily a whisper either. I wish I could say it was just like some Old Testament experience or that it equaled the magnitude of Paul's encounter with Jesus on the road to Damascus. But it wasn't like that. Instead, his voice was soft and subtle—almost monotone. I was in a quaint little coffeehouse reading some Scripture when my eyes fell onto these very familiar verses from Matthew 5:3–8 (NIV):

> Blessed are the poor in spirit, for theirs is the kingdom of heaven. Blessed are those who mourn, for they will be comforted. Blessed are the meek, for they will inherit the earth. Blessed are those who hunger and thirst for righteousness, for they will be filled. Blessed are the merciful, for they will be shown mercy. Blessed are the pure in heart, for they will see God. . . .

As I kept reading the words of Jesus from his "Mountain Sermon" in Matthew 5, I became sickened by the slavery I had allowed myself to seep into. All of my life I truly felt like I knew Jesus well—in fact, in my mind, I knew him extremely well. I had walked the aisle for the first time when I was four years old. I had gone to church three times a week for most of my life. I attended Bible studies. I sang in the choir. I worked with the youth group at my church. I was involved in it all—every church duty I could possibly dive into, I did. But his words in Matthew 5 suddenly made it evident to me that I had become so comfortable with my own flesh, my own condition, my own cage that I was failing to enjoy the freedom found in knowing Jesus. I thought that I knew Jesus. Now, looking back, I'm not sure he actually knew me. One verse that has always frightened me is the verse where Jesus said that on judgment day there will be those who scream "Lord, Lord," and his reply will be "I never knew you" (Matt. 7:22–23 NIV). I had cried out "Lord" every day for almost my entire life, but I was still enslaved.

I knew Jesus had died for my sins; I'd claimed that for twenty-two years. I believed it with all of my heart. But that day in the coffeehouse, I began to realize that I wasn't living a life of faith. I was living an imposter faith—something I had created, something I didn't even recognize.

The beautiful truth about provocative faith is that you cannot know Jesus and remain caged. It's spiritually impossible. Jesus hates it when his kids aren't free. He'll do whatever's necessary to release you from what ails you.

Freedom is no doubt the most important ingredient in living an extraordinary life of faith. Christians are limitless because they are free. Freedom is the very essence of our faith. We aren't able to fully love, be humble, and pursue evangelism without being free. Jesus came to our world to free us—to free us from our hopeless lives and to free us to pursue the calling that he has now placed on our lives.

Jesus is the basis of our freedom—that's why he shed his blood. But in order for us to embrace a free mindset, we need to believe in freedom with all of our hearts. We need people of all ages to ignore the world around them and focus every part of their being on the goals and dreams Jesus has set before them. Humans put too much emphasis on the cages of life. We often believe more in negativity and lies than we do in the freedom of Christ.

We have to be prepared for the challenges that lie ahead on the journey of provocative faith. We have to be ready to work through strongholds, to wage spiritual war against anything or anyone who challenges a Christian's freedom. These challenges may come in the form of legalism and rules, unbelief and ignorance, or unhealthy thinking about sin. When anything is added or taken away from the gospel of Jesus Christ, it's no longer the gospel—it's a lie keeping you from freedom. Cages manipulate. Cages remind us of our past. Cages don't just pull us away from freedom; they eliminate freedom. Sadly, people's faith often dies when their freedom is challenged.

What is your cage? Is it an unhealthy emotional tie to a friend? Is it fear of losing a loved one? Is it unconfessed sin that haunts your dreams? Is it simple doctrinal binds that weigh you down? Is it a person, place, or experience from the past that has you locked in chains? Only you know what keeps you from fully diving into a complete faith experience. No matter what it is, Jesus says be free. Jesus says blessed are those who hunger for what is good. Jesus says blessed are the ones with the pure heart. Jesus says that the truth will set you free. Do you believe wholeheartedly in the freedom of Christ?

One day while we were canoeing down a small river together, my friend Eileen Richardson told me about a book she had been reading. The book detailed the heinous conditions that missionaries endured while preaching the gospel message in Israel. After detailing all the spiritual needs and abuses many of these missionaries endured, she went on to tell me about the hungry and thirsty hearts that go without spiritual food because so few missionaries are there to teach them truth. Handing me the paddle for my turn at navigating us down the river, Eileen looked up at me and said, "Matthew, I believe God has called me to be a missionary in Jerusalem."

I was a prayer partner for Eileen as she waged her uphill battle to be a missionary in the Middle East. The odds were certainly stacked against her. This fifty-year-old, divorced mother of two was not the ideal candidate for missionary work. At least, that's what she was told. Her pastor said it was a long shot for a divorced mother to do any such thing. Her seminary professor told her that she should pursue children's work instead of missionary work. Her friends simply thought she was crazy for wanting to live in the Middle East during such tumultuous times. Even I was a bit skeptical—but hopeful. Eileen didn't care what others thought. She'd listen to them intently and then thank them for their opinion—but she always moved on, keeping her eyes and heart on Jesus. Eileen knew in her heart that she was called to be a missionary in Jerusalem, and that's what she intended to be.

She faced moments of discouragement—times when she felt depressed, unsure of her calling, and beaten up. But the grace of God sustained her. Every time she had a bad day, it only seemed to stoke the embers of her soul for her to keep pursuing her goal. Eileen didn't run away from the risks.

It was a long, hard battle, but after four years of missionary and counseling training at a seminary in Colorado, a year touring around the country to raise financial and prayer support, and many months of figuring out the basic logistics of moving to another country—a full six years after Eileen and I had that conversation in the canoe—she went to Jerusalem to teach and preach the gospel of Jesus to Jewish college students.

Eileen told me many times that her freedom in Christ was often her closest and only friend in her quest to become a missionary. "I refused to listen to the naysayers," she told me. "I don't play by the rules of the church or an individual. God called me to this position, and he is the one who gives me the freedom to go forward, not the church."

We all need Eileen's kind of freedom in Christ. It's contagious. She didn't listen to those who said a woman shouldn't be a missionary. She ignored the legalists who wouldn't support her financially because she was divorced. She was free of all that—free to pursue the dream God had for her.

We should all be so free.

One who is completely free in Christ knows he'll be maneuvering his way through many cages—experiences, people, and freedom-stealing fear—but he refuses to be defined by such things. I am reminded of this verse from the Gospel of John: "If the Son has set you free, then you are free indeed" (John 8:36 NIV). Embrace that freedom with all of your heart.

Freedom feels good, doesn't it?

Follower of Jesus finds faith strengthened despite abuse

One dark day when she was seven years old, a male babysitter sexually abused Julie Price. For more than twenty years, that event defined this friend of mine. Over the years, I have watched Julie come to grips with the reality of her past. She's shed countless tears. She's fallen into the depths of depression. She's become angry—at times her anger was so great that she physically ached. When Julie was twenty-two years old, she began to follow Jesus. But even after her conversion, the cage of guilt, anger, and pain still imprisoned her. For a very long time, freedom seemed distant and unattainable to Julie. I recently chatted with her about the battle to become free.

MT: First off, what exactly happened to you when you were a seven-year-old?

JP: I hate using the word *molested*—it sounds so dirty. But that's what happened. I was molested by a fourteen-year-old boy.

MT: Julie, at what age did you wake up and realize you were very angry about being sexually abused?

JP: When I was in high school, I was watching *Oprah* with my mother. The show was about people who had suffered abuse. I was so angry after watching that program that my mom said I should see a counselor.

MT: When did the anger begin?

JP: Oh, as a child. But I had repressed all of those feelings for so long that I did not recognize them as anger. But one day, it all began to surface. I suddenly realized that I had been violated. I realized that I was in emotional turmoil. And I believe one of the hardest parts of my entire story is that no professional doctor believed I was telling the truth. They thought I was making the whole thing up. That made me bitter.

MT: Tell me about your bitterness.

JP: I was angry because I was beginning to realize what that young man had done to me. He took a great deal of my childhood away from me. He took away my ability to love myself. Not only did he violate me, he took away my ability to trust the opposite sex. Still to this day, I have a hard time not keeping my relationships with guys at a safe arm's length.

MT: So the abuse damaged your self-esteem?

JP: Absolutely. In fact, I am still working through that. Up until last year, I had no idea that the abuse would have had any effect on my self-esteem. Because I had always struggled with being overweight and with being comfortable in my own skin, I never related the two.

MT: But eventually you connected the two, right?

JP: Right. I realized that I had turned my hatred for the individual who had done this to me into hatred toward myself. I loathed my body. It was nearly impossible to ever see myself as beautiful. It's hard not fitting society's image of beautiful. Two years ago, I started to see places where my many years of trying to avoid dealing with the abuse and my dwindling self-esteem were related.

MT: Did you have days when your feelings were more intense, more overwhelming?

JP: Oh gosh, yes. I never liked dealing with my feelings because it meant I had to relive the memory again. During the times I was trying to work through it—those times were horrible and scary.

MT: Scary?

JP: Yeah. At least, it was scary for me. I'll never forget the first time I went to therapy. [Julie laughs timidly.] I was a freshman in college, and I knew it was becoming quite obvious that I needed to seek help. I had started drinking heavily. I had begun dabbling in psychic stuff. I was a mess. When I sat down with the counselor to begin retelling my abuse story, I was terrified to have to face the reality of what occurred. I was literally shaking. Just the mere thought of what had happened made me physically ill—nauseous.

MT: You came to know Jesus when you were twenty-two. Did the abuse have anything to do with your decision to become a Christian?

JP: It had everything to do with it. During my senior year of college, I was actively pursuing counseling help. I had become so angry that I knew I had to deal with it. After I graduated, I tried analyzing myself, tried to get healthy on my own. For some reason I felt the need to read the Bible one night. I had many questions about Christ. So I asked one of my best friends about Jesus. By the end of that conversation, we were both down on our knees, and I was praying and asking Jesus to come into my life.

MT: After you came to know Jesus, was it easier to just forgive and forget?

JP: I don't believe I will ever forget what happened to me. Three years after I became a Christian, I went to see my pastor for counseling. My pastor validated my feelings. In other words, he made me feel "normal" and not stupid or silly for still feeling so much hatred toward the boy who did this. About three or four months after seeing my pastor, I began giving God my fear, anger, and hatred. I knew it was time to begin forgiving my abuser, and I have. But despite forgiving him, I won't forget what happened. I just don't live in the past any longer.

MT: Do you still think about what happened every day?

JP: You know, when I forgave him, I meant it. Of course, I still have moments when it comes to mind, but certainly not even close to every day.

MT: What have you learned about forgiveness through this situation?

JP: The ability to forgive comes from God—nowhere else. That's what I've learned.

MT: How has your faith grown from this experience?

JP: Before forgiveness, I was not dependent on God—now I am. I know now that I need God to get me through these tough situations. I have found such joy and freedom as a result of knowing God intimately. He is my Father, my sustainer, my peace. And I learned that he is willing to do anything— *anything*—in order to grow my faith. That's certainly scary sometimes, but I know that I am always better for it.

3

we must trust that God is good

As cliché as this might seem, a summer mission project in July 2000 proved to be an eye-opening experience for me. I say "cliché" because it seems that nearly every time a follower of Jesus goes on a missions experience, his or her life is changed in some way. But cliché or not, I believe such experiences do help us to grow in our understanding of Jesus, and these kinds of trips help to open our eyes to what a life of faith ultimately entails.

Seventeen eager individuals from my church left the comfort of our large, plush Northern Virginia homes and ventured to Cluj-Napoca, Romania, on a two-week mission trip. After spending a little over a week in the desolate Transylvania Alps with fifty or so fun, interesting, and smelly teenagers, our group visited a Romanian orphanage run by several strict Catholic nuns.

As our big, cream-colored school bus pulled into the circle drive of the orphanage, one of the orphans, a twelve-year-old boy named John, ran out to greet us. He was a spunky kid and kind of surprised us with his infectious energy.

"Welcome to Romania!" he said loud and clear, in near-perfect English as he grinned from ear to ear.

Truthfully, most of us had come to the orphanage prepared to be silent, solemn, and thoughtful. I think most of us expected the orphans to act like the children on those starving kid TV commercials with Sally Struthers. I don't think we expected the kids to be depressed—just not happy. We definitely weren't expecting such an exuberant welcome—especially from one of the kids.

"Do you know the song 'Jesus Loves Me'?" asked John loudly—*still* grinning. "Will you sing it with me?"

"Of course we know that song," someone said. We all began singing it loudly. It was a little awkward at first—like we were doing something incredibly uncool.

Jesus loves me, this I know . . .

As we sang the words of that children's song, a hundred thoughts ran through my mind. I stared at the orphan intently. One of his eyes was disfigured—like a birth defect. His hair was greasy and matted. His clothes were old and unmatched. He had a large, strange scar around his mouth—possibly from a botched surgery to correct a cleft palate.

For the Bible tells me so . . .

All of us on the bus had just been discussing our fear of getting head lice from the orphan kids. A couple of the girls were grossed out by the mere thought. A couple of them had asked if gloves were available. Don't they have special shampoo to kill head lice?

Little ones to him belong . . .

I thought about how happy my own childhood had been. I never had to wonder where I was going to sleep at night. I never went to bed hungry or in need of anything. My life was easy compared to what these orphans must face.

They are weak, but he is strong . . .

How could God allow a kid that he loves to be living in such heinous conditions? Is God really all that strong? Does he love us all the same? Is he good?

Yes, Jesus loves me.

Yes, Jesus loves me.

Yes, Jesus loves me. The Bible tells me so.

As we finished the last line, John hit a funny high note, making us all laugh. He laughed too. Maybe it was just because a group of American young people was there to play games with him and his friends, but John struck me as happy and even good—happier, in fact, than I am most of the time. John believed Jesus was good, and his circumstances somehow didn't refute that—they proved it. However, having faith in Jesus doesn't make situations like John's any easier to understand.

We got off the bus and toured the orphanage, playing games with the kids and hearing more about John's future. The orphanage only allows kids to remain through their thirteenth birthday. Most children have been at the orphanage all of their lives. Once they reach the "mature" age of thirteen, they are put out. And unless they're one of the lucky kids who find an adoptive parent to take them in, they end up living on the street. The director looked at us and said straightforwardly, "It would be impossible for us to handle children over the age of thirteen."

So because someone deems it impossible to care for a bunch of Romanian teenagers, John will probably be put out on the street and will likely have to steal for food, learning how to survive by committing crimes, sex acts, and in some cases violence. I would love for Jesus to come into John's situation and reveal himself the way I believe he should. But that's not how life works oftentimes.

John's story reminds me of a sermon I heard a pastor give last year about Jesus feeding of the five thousand. The pastor asked each individual to write down the dream or goal or event in his or her life that seemed impossible. He then compared the impossible task of Jesus feeding the five thousand with five loaves and two fishes to each of our impossible tasks. "Impossible," he said, "is nothing trusting God." Although I firmly and wholeheartedly believe that Jesus *can* come into any situation and heal it, solve it, make it, destroy it, or do it, he does not promise that he will. He expects us to trust him to know what is best for the lives of his children.

Despite the disparaging future that seems to be John's destiny, I must trust Jesus to know what is best. I don't trust because I understand him, or because I think he's going to do everything I ask of him, or because he is the God of miracles; I trust him because he promises his ways are good. But me trusting that God's good *is best* has not come easy. In fact, some days it's darn near impossible.

Our faith journey isn't always what we expect it to be. It's often ugly and messier than we hope. More often than not, it's harder than we anticipate. It's funny how you can be "on fire for Jesus" one moment and completely sideswiped the next by something that just doesn't make sense to you. Often we look for Jesus to intervene in our situations with his power and might and grace. And sometimes he does just that. But sometimes he chooses not to intervene—at least not in the way we expect him to. And in our finite minds, when Jesus does not respond to our situations by making our situations all better, our faith crumbles.

Most of us are quick to say that Jesus is good. But often *his* good and *our* expectations do not match. So instead of trusting his ways to be perfect and good, we get angry with him for not responding. Many of us even begin trying to work for Jesus's kindness. We spend our days trying to do God's will, hoping our good works will somehow guarantee that we will not be punished, or better yet, that they will ensure that we are blessed. Yet many of us end up disappointed—angry that we haven't seen God pull his weight in the miraculous. If I had been little Romanian John, I think I'd be more than a little angry.

Jerald Ferren, a man I knew when I was a child and respected well, came to know Jesus in the midst of filing for bankruptcy. This dad of seven kids walked into my church one day and surrendered his life to the pursuit of knowing Jesus. And Jerald instantly got involved in church work.

He started a ministry for the hearing impaired. He drove a bus to the needy neighborhoods of our community and picked up children whose parents would not bring them to church. He became an usher and a fill-in Sunday school teacher for my class. Everyone in the church agreed that Jerald's faith was growing by leaps and bounds.

But despite his newfound faith, Jerald's financial situation did not improve. In fact, it got worse. This was an irritation to Jerald. Subtly, his irritation became anger—anger toward Jesus for not fulfilling his end of the understood bargain. Little by little, Jerald began stepping away from his ministries. A little more than three years into his salvation experience, Jerald and his family left church altogether, saying it was a waste of time.

Apparently, Jerald brought his family to church and trusted that his good works would bring financial favor into his life. And you know what? For some Christians, it does work that way. We all know the stories of those who sacrificially give everything they have to the work of Christ, and they are blessed with five, ten, or twenty times their "investment." Much as I have treated God like an ATM for forgiveness and grace, others have treated him like he's a Wall Street broker—*I'll give you five, God; can you turn it into twenty?*

A few years ago, when Bruce Wilkinson's book *The Prayer of Jabez* became a *New York Times* best seller, I picked up the book and prayed the prayer a few times (I wasn't the only one who did either). Many of us picked up the habit of praying the prayer of Jabez in hope that some mysterious God-magic would happen in our lives. I expected blessing upon blessing to pour out on my life.

Bruce certainly made a killing of financial blessings off that prayer. I remember watching him on CNN as he boasted that his book was based on truth. *Whose truth?* I wondered. *Believe and be blessed? That's not really God's truth, is it?* But so many church leaders today lead their congregations astray with the bad theology that God will provide all that we want if we just believe. It's not simply Bruce Wilkinson. Many spiritual leaders would like for us to believe that all we have to do is simply ask God for anything, and he'll give it to us. Christian bookstores are full of books about this kind of stuff—prosperity and riches.

But under the radar screen, countless stories go untold of those who trust in Jesus with all they have and get little human wealth or gain in return. These stories aren't popular with many in the church. Such stories don't encourage new converts or encourage a congregation to "keep on keeping on." But these stories are real experiences in the lives of people with sincere faith in God. And I believe they tell a truer story of what it means to live a life of faith and a life of trust.

Many of today's churches like the success stories. We like to hear the stories about paupers who become CEOs and about cancer patients who eventually go into remission. We look for the stories about alcoholics who find Christ and never take another sip. We love to hear the stories about prostitutes who leave their profession behind once they hand their lives over to a loving God. We parade these individuals across the stages of our churches and cry, "This is the life of someone *trusting* in the power of Jesus." From these stories and examples, people end up trusting that Jesus will walk into their situation too—any situation—and make everything better.

How I wish the Christian life worked this way. Who *wouldn't* want to follow Jesus if it meant assured riches, blessings, good health, and success?

What do you say to the Christian alcoholic who can't say no to a drink? Is his faith any less? Can we not celebrate the miracle of Jesus's redemption if the individual returns to the bottle? Has this alcoholic stooped too far—out of reach of the miraculous, out of reach of grace? The church tells the alcoholic to trust God more. His Christian friends tell him to trust God more. His Christian counselor says with no doubt, "You're going to beat this, just trust more." The alcoholic puts every ounce of his energy into trusting Jesus—he thinks about Jesus, he reads his promises, he separates himself from the evilness of the world—but in the end, he takes another drink. I don't know about you, but I know that place all too well.

There have been many situations where instead of trust being an ongoing lifestyle I pursue, it's a means to an end. I think to myself, "I will trust in God through this situation in hopes that he will bring blessing upon my life." But this isn't trusting in Jesus; it's a mockery of trust. A person with provocative faith trusts in the middle of his situation—whether or not it's miraculously resolved. It's not an "if" faith but an "although" kind of trust that endures despite the situation. It's not a faith we hear proclaimed much on the stages of churches, but we can read it all through the Bible. "Though the cherry trees don't blossom," writes Habakkuk in his prophetic lament, ". . . though the apples are worm-eaten and the wheat fields stunted, though the sheep pens are sheepless and the cattle barns empty, I'm singing joyful praise to GOD. I'm turning cartwheels of joy to my Savior God" (Hab. 3:17–18).

It's so easy to tell ourselves that if God really loved us, he'd make our situations easy. But the truth is, our difficult situations show us that we're weak. And I think Jesus wants us to be weak. He can use the weak. Jesus wants his followers to be at a place where our ability to trust in ourselves is completely destroyed and no longer available. Proverbs 3:5 says to trust in God with all of your being and not to depend on your own ridiculous thought process. A Christian has the responsibility to trust Jesus with everything that he or she is. But Scripture quickly follows that request with a challenge to not rely on the thoughts, actions, beliefs, and statements of humanity. As Christians we must get to the place where we simply trust Jesus to know more than we do.

God is not the fairy godmother; he's not a genie in a bottle. It's easy to get caught up in the belief that God wants to bless me beyond my understanding. And the people who sell these beliefs are often dynamic individuals who are masters at selling their point of view to a weary public. As much as I see God move in my life, I don't believe he cares what car I drive or how big my house is or what is or isn't in my bank account. Especially when people exist in this world who are right now wondering where their next meal is going to come from. Jesus said that the first will be last in the kingdom of heaven. In light of his words, why would God waste his time making all of us first in line?

No guarantee for twentysomething couple who trusts God for baby?

David and Elisabeth Banks know all too well about the pain and frustration that go into trusting God. For four years they have tried to get pregnant, with no success. She's been tested; everything seems to be fine. He's been tested; everything seems to be normal. The doctors told them to just calm down and keep trying. That's what they did—for more than two years. But the more they tried, the more consumed they became with having a baby. And the more consumed they became, the harder it was to simply trust. I interviewed David and Elisabeth two weeks after they invested thousands of dollars in the procedure known as in vitro fertilization.

MT: Elisabeth, let me start with you—when did you start getting worried that you might not be able to get pregnant?

EB: I was worried six months after I went off birth control. I never expected to have a problem. My mom and sisters never experienced problems getting pregnant. I expected to get pregnant right away.

DB: But in all honesty, Lis has always been the one to worry. She's known for her worrying. [Both laugh.]

EB: It's true; I am.

MT: Had you told others you were trying to have a baby?

EB: Not really. I mean, I told my mom and a couple other members of the family, but that's pretty much it. And even when we realized that getting pregnant was going to be a problem, we still kept it to ourselves for the most part.

MT: When did you decide it was time for you to go see a doctor?

DB: About a year and a half after we went off birth control.

EB: We figured something must be wrong with us. A few years before, David had experienced some minor health problems with his bladder; I thought it must have something to do with that.

MT: But when you both went to get checkups, the doctors didn't find any reason why you shouldn't get pregnant, right?

EB: Not anything major. I mean, there were a couple smaller things that came up in the testing that might have been a cause. But doctors were still very hopeful.

DB: The doctors didn't see any reason why we shouldn't be getting pregnant naturally.

MT: During this time, what was going on with you emotionally?

EB: Honestly, I was a wreck. I was stressed, probably a little depressed, but still, I was trying to function to the best of my ability.

DB: I think the hard part was that every couple around us was having babies. All of our friends were either pregnant or had newborns. That was hard, especially for Lis.

EB: It got to the point that I hated to go to church or to a party or to any kind of gathering for fear that someone would tell me they were expecting. And at times, even being around others' babies was hard. One time I was in a circle of friends when one of them blurted out, "Guess what? I'm pregnant." I literally thought I was going to vomit. Crying, I left the party.

MT: David, why wasn't it as hard for you?

DB: I kept telling myself, *When God wants us to have a baby, we'll have a baby.*

EB: Yeah, David was a lot more positive than me. He has been a pillar through all of this.

MT: What were you both saying to God during this time?

EB: We were praying faithfully every night. I was telling God what he already knew—that I wanted a baby.

DB: We asked him a lot of questions too.

MT: Did you doubt?

EB: Oh, I did. There were many times when I was so angry with God I could have screamed. Every month when I got my period, it felt like I had experienced another punch in the stomach.

63

DB: I didn't doubt. It's not necessarily my nature to doubt. But it was very hard watching Lis struggle. It was putting a lot of strain on our marriage.

MT: Is that when you decided to seek out an alternative method?

EB: Yeah. After two and a half years of trying, we both decided it was time to go get some help. Everyone was telling us to pray harder. Everyone was giving us advice. I was so sick of hearing people remind me of the "Hannah asking God for a baby" story from the Bible. And I know everyone meant well, but we didn't want to hear words—we wanted a baby.

DB: And when you're going through things like this, people say the dumbest things. Lis came home one night and just fell on the couch and cried because someone who knew what we were going through spent the entire evening telling stories about her baby.

MT: So you were tired of people telling you to "just trust."

EB: Definitely. We *were* trusting God to know what was best, but I think people expect you not to hurt through the process— that simply because you know Jesus has your best in mind, that you're supposed to be happy all of the time. And that's just not the case.

(The conclusion of this interview is at the end of chapter 4.)

4

the burning bush
isn't for everyone

The entire church had been praying for a miracle. Dixon
Michaels was sick—very sick. Doctors expected him to die.
But my church expected a miracle. We expected the good
God of the universe to reveal himself in this situation and
make this man well. After all, Jesus was always healing the
sick—that's what he did—he was the Great Physician.

We had special prayer services for Dixon. The pastor,
deacons, and elders laid hands on him and asked Jesus
to heal. One man even anointed Dixon's forehead with
oil. We begged, pleaded, and wrestled with God over
Dixon's life. And most in the church fully expected God
to respond.

In the end, despite the prayers, the laying on of hands, and the oil, Dixon died.

Making the mistake of basing my Christian life on books and the spiritual whims of man, I've wasted a great deal of time waiting on God to perform miracles on my behalf. This is not to say that I have never experienced miracles. We all experience miracles. But miracles and blessings come in many different packages and usually appear very differently than we expect.

Like many of you reading this book, I have prayed, begged, negotiated, and bartered with God so many times for him to perform, generate, lengthen, and expand. But it often seems God doesn't answer. And most of us get discouraged.

For some people, the idea that waiting on God could be a waste of time might be an uncomfortable concept to admit or even blasphemous to utter out loud. I do *not* believe that waiting on God is a waste, but waiting on him to perform on my behalf, in the way I expect, definitely is. And I've wasted more than my share of precious time waiting on God to awe me with a miraculous sign to prove to me that he is indeed in control, or at least is doing *something* on my behalf.

Of course, there have been times when my eyes have gazed upon poverty in third-world nations or on inner-city streets and I've longed for God to perform a miracle. I've watched natural disasters such as tornadoes, earthquakes, and tsunamis steal the soul away from a country or city or home, and I've expected to see God's hand respond to the crisis. And as I've watched a loved one who was sick lay dying in a hospital bed, I expected God to heal—and heal quickly. But more often than not, as I watched these types of situations in hope-filled horror, God chose not to respond the way I was certain he would. Or he simply responded in ways I don't understand, in ways that my limited comprehension of his goodness just didn't get. Does this make God not good? Does this make him uncaring? Does this make him an unengaged bystander unwilling to help me? I don't believe so.

Many people of faith wait patiently (and some *impatiently*) for God to intervene at just the right time—but too often, our limited understanding of his ways leaves us believing that the *right* time never comes. In the meantime, children die, families go bankrupt, terrorists kill, the guilty go free, and thousands of people are left to mourn the loss of human life, dignity, and passion. Many of us look at these situations and think it's unjust. I look at these situations and ask, "Why, God?"

During my times of waiting, I wasn't necessarily in need of a burning bush to speak out loud or a cloud of fire to lead me around the wilderness at night. But I was certainly looking for God to wow me with something that would let me know that he was involving himself in my life—that his hand was somewhere in close proximity to guide me through this messed-up world. I wasn't picky either. One of his smaller signs or wonders would have worked just fine. When you're looking for a miracle from God, you're usually desperate, so any sign to let you know that he exists will usually do. And when I didn't see the miraculous, I looked to Scripture for some inspiration.

The Bible is filled with stories about people of faith who encountered a miraculous God. Such stories have been used to explain God's providence for centuries. Pastors and priests have repeated these stories to help followers of God remain faithful—at any cost. And the church doesn't shy away from reminding us of these stories when we're in the midst of pain either. When you're facing loss or depression, everyone tells you about Job. When a young couple aches to get pregnant, we quickly mention the story of Hannah. When we know Christians facing temptation, doubt, and tribulation, we faithfully remind these followers about God's miraculous dealings with Abraham, David, and Joseph. There's no shortage of stories to remind us that God does indeed do miracles.

When we don't have others to remind us of those powerful stories of faith, we remind ourselves of their meaning in our lives. I can't tell you how many times I've taken miraculous stories from Scripture out of context and related them to my own life.

A few years ago, I was on the verge of running out of the medication I take for acid reflux. At the time, I had no insurance. I had no money to pay full price for the drugs. Without the help of insurance, who can afford paying four dollars a pill? As I got closer and closer to an empty prescription bottle, I began praying that God would provide.

I reminded myself of how God provided for the widow of Zarephath and her son in 1 Kings 17. God had told the prophet Elijah to stop at a widow's house and ask her for some bread. Elijah did so. But the widow said that she only had enough flour and oil for one more loaf of bread, and then she and her son would soon die of starvation. Elijah told the poor widow that if she would have faith and make him a loaf of bread, God would provide enough flour and oil for her to make another loaf. The widow had faith; she made Elijah some bread, and when she returned to her flour container and oil jar, God had provided her with enough of both for another loaf of bread. As it turned out, because of the widow's faith, God continued to provide flour and oil for her and her son until the rains returned.

As I read about how God had provided for the widow, I thought this would be an amazing time for him to reveal his presence to me through my need for more medication.

When I finally reached in to grab the last pill, I truly expected there to be one more pill in the container the next morning when I went to my medicine cabinet. But to my disappointment, there was no pill. It was empty.

Come on, God, I thought. *You're supposed to know my needs even before I do. Why can't you give me one darn pill to help me?* So I bartered with God. I told him that if he would supply me with this one little miracle, I would let everyone I knew hear of his goodness toward me.

I wish I could tell you that the *next* day I woke up to a free pill in my medicine cabinet—but alas, all I woke up to was heartburn.

I did get a little discouraged, but I chalked my dilemma up to not having enough faith. In fact, every time God didn't respond to my begging, it was always because I did not have enough faith in him. So I'd try harder and expect more. And even though I was pretty sure my faith in God was at least the size of a mustard seed (I'm not sure how you really measure things like this), more often than not, I saw no mountains moving, no bush burning, and no extra Prevacid in my medicine cabinet.

Many of us have been discouraged by God's apparent disinterest in our circumstances. There is nothing more disheartening than to hear an individual express their doubt in God because he did not perform the way they thought he should. We hear preachers teach on the miracles of Jesus; we believe in the miracles of Jesus and truly expect him to come through for us. But so many times, the cancer comes back, the child still dies, and the bank account remains empty, leaving us feeling very alone and befuddled by the inexplicable goodness of God.

One who lives a life of centralized faith in Jesus certainly knows the truth that God *is* good—quite good. But that same person is constantly at war with his temptation to define God's goodness in earthly terms or with a human equation. We cannot lower God to the sums of our sub-standard concepts of good. They will never equal or even be close. Those who are disappointed or frustrated by the actions of God are almost always guilty of boxing their concepts of God.

I have often heard self-proclaimed postmodern preachers tell their congregations that many Christians are guilty of putting *God* in a box. I've used the God-in-a-box terminology myself a few times. But truly, the thought is preposterous. You cannot be guilty of boxing up a God who cannot be contained. It's as if we're saying that it's actually possible to limit God. You can't limit an omnipotent God. You can only limit your openness to the breadth of God. Jesus knew this, and it is why he talked to his disciples about how they should anticipate the actions of God in their daily lives. And we must trust his words.

Jesus said in Luke 12:27–28 (NLT):

> Look at the lilies and how they grow. They don't work or make their clothing, yet Solomon in all his glory was not dressed as beautifully as they are. And if God cares so wonderfully for flowers that are here today and gone tomorrow, won't he more surely care for you? You have so little faith!

Jesus says that just as his Father clothes the lily with bright color and douses it with alluring perfume, God will do that and more for his children.

Again in Matthew 6:32–34 (NLT), part of Jesus' Sermon on the Mount, he addresses these same concerns:

> Your heavenly Father already knows all your needs, and he will give you all you need from day to day if you live for him and make the Kingdom of God your primary concern. So don't worry about tomorrow, for tomorrow will bring its own worries.

In the years when Jesus was 100 percent human and 100 percent sovereign, he tasted the fear we humans cling to that God is complacent in our lives. He too was tempted to fear God's seeming complacency in his own life. On the cross, Jesus cried out toward heaven, "Why have you forsaken me?" Jesus's words portrayed his own terror that God had somehow left him. But Jesus addressed that kind of fear; he did not leave us stranded. I believe he realized how easily our faith can be pulled astray when we doubt whether God cares for the human race. Jesus was the ultimate evidence that God always has our best interest in mind. But, of course, God does not promise that we'll understand his ways or be able to demand a miraculous performance. He says we must simply trust him. And that is difficult—often overwhelmingly so.

I do believe God is merciful toward our unbelief. But he longs to pull us out of our jaunt of mediocre faith and allow us to see that he is trustworthy, faithful, and always good—always. We must trust this.

I've often been jealous of God's work in the lives of others. He seemingly speaks and moves all day long in the lives of some believers. But I've learned that in my pursuit of provocative faith in God, I must never look at the way God is dealing in the life of others and wish him to do the same in my life. Like Jesus said many times, God knows what I need. My needs are different than yours. Your needs are different than your pastor's. Do not look at the lives of others and compare. That's not faith.

Often we say we're trusting God, but instead of trusting for his best, we're looking for him to provide a particular outcome to our experience. And when we trust him for a specific event to occur or a circumstance to happen, we really aren't trusting at all. We're hoping, wishing—but not trusting. We're telling God what to do instead of asking him for his ultimate goodness to be revealed.

God is good. We may not always understand his goodness, but we must learn to keep our hearts and minds open to the truth that Jesus understands us. He knows how our minds work, but he also knows what we need—truly need. And that alone is miraculous enough for me to believe.

No guarantee for twentysomething couple who trusts God for baby?

(Interview continued from chapter 3.)

MT: Elisabeth and David, what strengthens you during this time?

DB: The support of family and friends is unbelievable. Knowing that there are countless people praying for us is a huge blessing. But ultimately, we've had to learn to trust God—that he knows what's good.

MT: How did you learn that?

EB: We have to go back to what we know to be truth. We have to remind ourselves of the basic attributes of God—his love, mercy, and grace. That's not to say it's still not difficult—because it is, but God continues to be patient with us and teach us what it means to trust.

DB: We also have to rely on each other. Sometimes when Lis is weak, I need to be her strength, and vice versa.

MT: So you went to a birthing clinic, and what did they do?

EB: They ran a hundred different blood tests on both of us, but especially me. About a month after our visit, the doctor told us that we could proceed with artificial insemination.

MT: And basically, that's a procedure where they take David's sperm and manually place it inside you, right?

EB: [They smile at each other.] It's a little embarrassing to talk about, but yes, that's what it is. But before we could do this, I had to take many different medications to prep my body for the surgery. Some of the meds were hormones, which certainly wreaked havoc on my emotions.

DB: Yes, they did. It was horrible. Lis was more emotional and teary than ever before.

MT: What happened?

EB: The procedure didn't work. I was devastated when I got the news. I had gotten my hopes up, and literally, when the doctor told me that I wasn't pregnant, it felt like someone had died. I didn't know what to do.

DB: It was very disappointing. This is when it started hitting us both the same. Up until then I had always been the strong one, but we both were hurting.

EB: We ended up doing that procedure three different times. On the second time, I miscarried very early on.

MT: What was going through your mind at that time?

DB: The worst part of this whole thing has been the ups and downs. We would get our hopes up, take every precaution, and then it wouldn't work.

EB: After the third time, I was ready to give up. I was ready to just pursue adoption. I thought that obviously God didn't want us to have a baby. I was selfish, angry, and at my wits' end.

MT: Let's fast-forward a few months. You didn't give up. You decided you wanted to have in vitro. Can you explain to me exactly what that is?

DB: In vitro in laymen's terms is this: The doctor takes the egg out of the female and sperm out of the male and brings the two together to create a healthy embryo. And then, after five days, the embryo is placed in the uterus.

MT: Some Christians might say that pursuing this procedure means that you're not trusting. How do you respond to that?

EB: Well, if that person had seen how God brought this whole thing together, I don't believe they would respond that way. First off, we prayed and asked God for wisdom with all of this. We didn't just do it. There were so many hoops to jump through—insurance, finances, timing—and even after doing it, there was still a chance that it might not work. We had to think about it all. I had to really pray about whether or not I was emotionally strong enough to go through this.

MT: And you decided that you were, right?

EB: Yes.

DB: We had come this far; I don't believe we could have turned back now. We felt called to have children. We watched God put us in the hands of the best doctors. We watched him provide the insurance and the finances. We felt like it was his will for us to move forward.

MT: Allow me to be blunt and ask this: are you prepared for this procedure not to work?

EB: I've thought about that a lot. I don't think you're ever prepared for God to say no. But I can say this: I've told him that I will learn to be content with whatever he decides is best.

DB: We have to get up each morning and make a point to trust God again. It's not something that comes naturally for humans. I have to get down on my knees and ask God for the faith to trust him.

EB: Unfortunately, every day is a little different. Some days I wake up and I am happy and strong; other days I am preoccupied with what I want and what I need and I am weak. It doesn't mean that I am not trusting in God for his best; it means I am still not content with his answer. But my desire is to be content.

DB: We've learned through this process that God is faithful. He is with us, and he will do what he wants to make us more like him.

Update: Three weeks after our interview, David and Elisabeth found out they were expecting twins. Siera Nichole and Emma Katherine were born on April 21, 2005.

5

pride always makes you look fat— very fat

In the first two chapters of this book, I retold the story of how God woke me up from my personal cage. He showed me my sadistic concept of grace and forgiveness. But fortunately, God didn't just leave me there to sulk in my own self-pity. He began to teach me more about myself. He began to ask me to move out of my own selfishness and into a life of humility. And the first step to pursuing humility is to know one's self. We must know our flaws and our mistakes before we can truly be humble. We must confess to God who we really are before he can begin to build us back up and use us.

After being sideswiped by Jesus' Sermon on the Mount, I left the coffeehouse that day with fervor to know more about what it truly means to have *faith* in God. My step seemed lighter. My heart felt freer. It seemed like I was floating on some spiritual cloud. I had this overwhelming sense that the next few days would be a profound time of listening for me and remaining very still and quiet before God. He had finally spoken, and although I expected that it was going to be a long uphill climb to understanding exactly who God was, I felt somehow readied for the endeavor. But then God spoke again and woke me up from my silly little Jesus dream and showed me how wrong I was. I wasn't ready for any uphill climb—not even close—and I was definitely not ready for what was to come next.

Over those next few days, God began to speak. Oh, some don't believe God speaks today, but I believe that he does. I've heard him. People may consider me a lunatic for telling such a tale, but I'd be foolish not to. During this time, God woke me up in the middle of the night and put Scripture on my mind to read. He sent friends over to reveal truth to me. His voice rang loud and clear in my mind, heart, and soul—not always audibly loud—but hearable nonetheless. As many might assume, it's not always grand to hear God speak. I cried. I screamed. I begged. I threw fits. I got depressed. I got silent. I got humble. God started breaking my life apart.

God kicked me in my butt so many times that I thought his grandiose foot was going to end up lodged somewhere between my pancreas and my left kidney. Churches are always quick to talk about the mercy, grace, and kindness of God, but they rarely mention the sting of his retribution and how that feels against your backside. And while he's no doubt faithful, comforting, loving, and all of that, he also knows how to kick your spirit into another gear altogether. And he spent a good deal of time working me over like I was a puny freshman on my first day of high school.

When I left that coffeehouse, I was grinning from ear to ear with mystical anticipation of what was to come, but God quickly *and* emphatically began to put me in my place. I came to realize that I had more emotional and spiritual baggage than I first expected. I imagine that this experience might have felt a little like the time Jesus stormed into the temple and knocked over sales tables and then rebuked the moneychangers. He stormed into my heart—one of his personal temples—and began knocking down the walls of deceit, judgment, codependency, religion, and everything else I held too tightly.

It's my experience that God will do just about anything necessary to get you where he wants you to be. One of my favorite biblical stories is Jonah's refusal to go to Nineveh. I like this story because I see so much of myself in Jonah. He blatantly told God that he did not want to go and preach to Nineveh. Jonah's retreat away from God's plan landed him on a boat. I've heard preachers and teachers wonder why God didn't choose someone else. That isn't God's nature. He refuses to let our disobedience keep him from chasing after what he desires. In God's mind Jonah was going to Nineveh whether he liked the concept or not. God followed Jonah onto that boat; he showed up in the wind, lightning, rain, and waves. He also showed up in the casting of lots—for Jonah ended up getting the short one. And then God revealed himself through the presence of a large fish. And after Jonah spent some time sitting in the belly of that fish, he did indeed go to Nineveh and in a sense preached the gospel.

God wants *us* flat on our faces before him. He wants us to get comfortable with a couple of hard words: submit and surrender. Looking back, I realized that so much of my life was not completely humbled to the gospel of Christ. He is willing to do whatever's necessary to get us where he wants us to be. A person of provocative faith lets him have his way.

Often when we first meet Jesus, we are so mesmerized by the experience that we fail to realize that a relationship with him takes time to develop. I often equate it to falling in love with your significant other. Sometimes people fall in love without truly getting to know each other and without appreciating the differences that each person brings into the relationship. We end up spending our days trying to mold the person into our idea of the perfect match. I've been there. When my wife, Jessica, and I first met, I constantly tried to make her into exactly what I thought I needed in a wife instead of trusting that God's gift to me was exactly what I needed, ordained by him.

Many of us come into a relationship with God through Jesus with the same problem. Instead of enjoying this new relationship and gradually getting to know what the gift of salvation truly holds, we instantly begin molding it and letting others mold it into what we/they think is needed. Many of us have so many years of experience molding God that we hardly remember what it feels like to let God mold us. That kind of molding, where God does the work on us, begins with humility—humility to the sacrifice Jesus endured on the cross. Before we can live a life defined by

80

humility, we must first come to the realization that our lives are pointless and meaningless without that sacrifice. I have to come back to that truth again and again, or I begin to take my life back into my hands. The words of Christ must keep bringing all of us back to humility.

Jesus said that in our weakness we are made stronger. Jesus said that in the kingdom of God, the first will be last and the last will be first. Jesus said that if someone asks you to walk with him a mile, walk with him two. Jesus said to love your neighbor as you love yourself, but more importantly, love your enemies. Jesus said the humble will be exalted.

Such thoughts and perspectives from Christ fly in the face of everything we've ever been taught by our society. Jesus is describing the antihero of today's culture. Think about it. If Spiderman didn't win at the end of the movie, if he wasn't right about the bad guy, would millions of people really want to watch? Would Jason Bourne from *The Bourne Identity* be as cool and impressive if he loved his enemies instead of killing them? Do we celebrate good losers at the Olympics? Does Adidas endorse the player who spends most of his time sitting on the bench? Does the humble candidate win a presidential election? And when it comes to size, is smaller really better?

You might be thinking to yourself, *But these are mostly "worldly" examples.* And that's true. But the same mindset exists in Christian culture too. I'm not writing this book to slam the church, though all of us can see for ourselves where pride has seeped into the doctrine and culture of many churches around the world. I'm more concerned for the individual.

What about the nature of our own hearts? Are we pursuing the lifestyle of humility? If a person knows Jesus, he or she is expected to always pursue the humble route as opposed to the road everyone else travels.

Sometimes I question whether or not we actually believe those hard teachings of Jesus. Could it truly be that the last will be first or the humble will be exalted? That is what Jesus said. Do you believe it? Are you willing to bank your faith on being humble?

An individual who understands the teachings of Jesus is willing to get naked without being ashamed. He's willing to bare all in order to let God have his way. He isn't consumed by the expectations of man; he's focused on becoming more like Jesus. Jesus wants his followers to pursue humility; it's a prerequisite for provocative faith.

Exactly two months before we were to be married, my future wife and I were in the middle of a heated discussion. Okay, let's call it what it was: a fight. Jessica expressed her frustration over my seemingly careless attitude toward an issue that touched her deeply. Getting tired of confrontation, I did what most guys do and just shut down—only responding to her with a few selfish comments here and there. I couldn't comprehend why my fiancée was so moved by something that I thought was small and irrelevant, and so our little "discussion" continued for more than an hour. Words, thoughts, and opinions went round and round, back and forth between us until we were both worn out and about to retreat to our separate corners without resolution.

After a few moments of silence spent scanning my brain and heart for the answer to our disagreement, God gave me the strength to be humble. In the midst of battling over an important concern of Jessica's, I realized that the only thing I wanted out of the conversation was to be right while Jessica only wanted me to understand her point of view. And I wanted to be right. Jessica desired that I be concerned for how this situation was making her feel. And I just wanted to be right. Jessica wasn't trying to hurt me by bringing this issue to the surface; she only wanted freedom from her weighted mind—and I wanted to be right.

We all crave being right sometimes. Being right is the best feeling in the world. It's empowering. Being right makes us feel strong, in control, and good about ourselves. It's a shot of adrenaline to an individual's ego and pride. When we're right, people notice us, our opinion matters, and everyone will shut up and listen to us. In our minds we think, *No one gets to the pedestal being wrong or weak or the last in line.* We have to be first. We have to win. It's the game we play with ourselves inside our heads. Being right ultimately makes us feel a little godlike. It takes the victory away from God and places it squarely on our own ability, our actions.

Today's culture is full of people who live their lives with the ultimate goal of being right. We lie to be right. We end relationships to be right. We go into war against each other to be right. Some of us want to be right no matter what the cost. It doesn't matter who gets knocked down on the road to being right, we just want someone to look at us in the end and say, "Okay, I give up, you're right."

There's nothing wrong with being right. It's the attitude that often comes along with being right that is the problem. When Jessica and I were fighting, I might have been right about the issue being petty or ridiculous. But my attitude toward her and toward her feelings grew out of my desire to simply prove her wrong. Jesus can't fully use an individual who must always prove himself or herself right.

In Scripture, James writes, "God sets himself against the proud, but he shows favor to the humble" (James 4:6 NLT). God desires his people to pursue humility. A major discovery for me in my pursuit of provocative faith was understanding my need for a spirit of humility and how I must fight against my nature to be proud, envious, materialistic, and always right.

A good friend of mine visited Haiti several years ago. He returned to the United States with many questions regarding what it means to be last in the kingdom of God. This trip had touched him deeply. He spoke of trash-laced streets, starvation run amuck, and dumpy shacks that families of eight or more call their homes. He had always known that he was *far* from last when it came to financial matters. He lived in the United States. He had a house, a job, and good food. But the sight of people living in such troubled conditions reminded him of what Jesus said about being last, and frankly, that scared him.

"If the last are going to be first, then I'm in trouble," he said to me over coffee one afternoon.

"What do you mean?" I asked.

"Matthew, looking at those kids' lives and comparing their experiences to my own frightened me. I might as well be first in line. I've got everything I could ever want.

And I really wouldn't know how to get rid of any of it. And instead of understanding what Jesus meant when he said the first will be last, I'm confused now as to what he meant by that statement."

I understand my friend's fear. He got me thinking about what it truly means to be last and how it relates to my faith. I hate the concept of being last. It's lonely at the end of any line. Being last is one of those hard teachings of Christ that frankly befuddles me at times. But it's a teaching we all need to wrestle with and understand before we can truly know the Father.

Only a few short days before Mother Teresa passed away, the world lost one of its most beloved and worshiped individuals of my lifetime: Princess Diana. I can remember exactly where I was when I heard the news of Diana's passing. With the media frenzy surrounding Princess Diana's tragic, complicated death, many hardly noticed that just a few days later, the world lost a true princess. But just as Mother Teresa lived a life of humility, so she died humbly too. It was a beautiful final chapter to a story that lives on in the hearts of so many whom Mother Teresa touched with her kindness. Mother Teresa's impact on India has been discussed, heralded, and covered to death. But still, the little nun who lived most of her life in Calcutta among the poor seemed to understand this notion of being last. And while the world was watching the controversial death of Princess Diana, a ninety-year-old woman who gave her life to charity passed into eternity. I like to imagine that Mother Teresa's eternal welcome was a grand parade of events only overshadowed by the glory of Jesus himself. I do hope she's in the front of the line somewhere.

But how do we pursue being last? I don't believe we need to sell our houses and cars, leave our current jobs, and move to the slums of a third-world nation to have a "last place" perspective. I don't believe we all need to move to India and live like Mother Teresa to be able to think with the last in mind. I believe faith teaches us that it's more about our motives, our mindset, and how we live our lives in response to the gospel of Jesus Christ that makes us "last." The men and women who run homeless shelters *surely* know what it means to be last, but I believe you can also be a celebrity of sorts or the CEO of a Fortune 500 company and still pursue being last. "Last" might be found in an individual's leadership style, community mentality, or how he or she develops and appreciates relationships. It's an ongoing process to be last.

Being last is a mindset to be pursued. As followers of Jesus, we have to constantly go back to the gospel message and realize again and again that we are nothing without Jesus's blood covering on our lives. It's realizing that everything in life must go through the filter of Jesus for us to truly understand what it means to be people of faith. Provocative faith doesn't answer to politics and banter, pop culture and philosophy; it stands alone on the very truth of Jesus. And he said that the first *will* be last and the last *will* be first in his kingdom.

God awoke me to my own "I want to be first" mentality two years ago when I found myself completely consumed with the success and influence of a job. Yes, a job. You might think this ridiculous, but don't get too high-and-mighty; many of us are cramming to be first in line professionally. I certainly tried, but then God stepped in and whacked my pride down to size.

When I was the editor of *CCM* magazine, the largest Christian music publication in the world, I was making $65,000 a year doing a job that I adored. When I took the position, many questioned whether or not I was qualified for the job (heck, when I considered that I only had eight months of editorial experience at a dot com and a business administration degree, I questioned it myself). I told God that I couldn't do any of this without his help, and he was going to have to surround me with people who knew more than I did about editing. And then I worked hard, dead set on proving my critics wrong. Sure enough, God did put people in my life who helped me climb this impossible "mountain." But at some point I took God out of my mental equation. I got cocky and actually started thinking I could do the job on my own. My boss saw this. My co-workers saw this. I saw this. I ignored it. They didn't.

But no matter; I continued to pour more and more of my life into that job. I cherished the financial benefits of working there. I bought a condo. I bought an engagement ring and made plans to be married. I splurged on a few things that I didn't need. To a music-business major who desired to be successful and influential in the Christian music industry, that job was a dream come true. And so I foolishly built a large part of my existence around that position at *CCM*.

Two years into my position, I was fired.

Wait just a minute, I thought. *Matthew Paul Turner is never "let go" from a job. He bows out gracefully by choice when another opportunity comes along. He doesn't get fired!*

Getting fired from *CCM* was a blow to every part of my being—my pride, my standing as a respected leader in Nashville, and my pocketbook. In my mind, I went from holding one of the most respected jobs in the Christian music industry to being nothing. I felt like I had lost it all. Sure, that's a dramatic way of putting it, but that's exactly how I felt.

It's these kinds of circumstances that remind us of our personal priorities. Remember when I said God would do whatever was necessary in your life to get you where he wants you to be? Well, this was one of those situations for me. *Bam!* As quickly as I had gotten that job, I lost it.

I realize now that God wasn't overly impressed with my job at *CCM*. I'm sure he was glad that I enjoyed it. But impressed by it? No. It wasn't sinful for me to have a job that I enjoyed. God desires us to enjoy our lives. But in my case, he knew that I had lost my dependence on him. He watched me step up onto a pedestal and think I could do it alone. He was hardly impressed that I had built my entire life of influence and success around that ridiculous job. God was more concerned about my heart; he was concerned that my entire world wasn't built around him. So he took it from me. Actually, he kind of snatched it from me. I grew up being taught that snatching was impolite, but I guess God didn't care.

I would love to be able to tell you that I kept my composure that day when I found out from my boss that the company was letting me go. But that would be a lie—and actually, a really big one. I cried and screamed like a baby that day. I said a word about thirteen times that I can't even print here—and felt completely justified in doing so. But ultimately, I was silenced, put in my place, and humbled. I'd be misleading you if I didn't say that my faith in God felt a little beaten up by all of this.

Situations that leave you feeling like you're standing in front of a large crowd with your pants down are indeed humbling. And I would love to start telling you now that getting fired from my job was the best thing that could have happened to me and that God just worked everything out perfectly for my good. But I'm not going to do that. I'm not sure it would be true. And anyway, that's not what faith is all about. I survived the firing. And I certainly learned a very humbling lesson. But more than anything, I learned that God always gets his way. We can move with him gracefully or we can go kicking and screaming, but all of us eventually get to where he wants us to be. The faith journey is a constant lesson in the art of moving with him gracefully and willingly and always. Faith is letting the other guy get in line in front of you. A person who has faith trusts the truth that God will lift up the humble and diminish the proud.

Being last is an ugly lesson at times. But it's one that all of us must endure. Jesus hates pride. He will do whatever's necessary to knock us off our pedestals and onto the ground before him.

Young man humbled;
loses everything because of affair

Twenty-nine-year-old Cameron Briggs (not his real name) gets choked up talking about his divorce. His marriage of three years ended abruptly two years ago when his twenty-six-year-old wife discovered that he was having an affair with another married woman at his office. Not only did Cameron lose his marriage, but he also lost his job. His answers during my interview are short, honest, and to the point. I included this interview in this book because I believe it reveals an honest picture of what being humbled can feel like.

MT: Cameron, tell me how you met your wife.

CB: I met my wife at a bank in Chicago. She actually helped me secure the loan for my house. I asked her out soon after that. We got married a year and a half later. My wife is a beautiful woman. She loved me with all of her heart.

MT: Would you consider your marriage to have been happy?

CB: I think so. Of course, we had problems just like everyone else, but for the most part our marriage was happy. We never stayed mad at each other. People considered us to be the "perfect couple." At church, we were always one of the couples chosen to have our picture taken for church promo shots. We looked good, I guess.

MT: Were you both active in your church?

CB: We were very active. My wife volunteered for everything. She was a nursery worker. She also taught a preschool Sunday school class. I helped out with the church youth program and sang on the worship team about once a month.

MT: And you also worked at a local Christian ministry in Chicago, right?

CB: Yes, that's right. I worked at a large church as a graphic designer.

MT: The woman you had an affair with also worked at this church, correct?

CB: She did. We shared an office with another male employee.

MT: Cameron, when you met this woman, were you looking to have an affair?

CB: Yes and no. Yes, I was certainly lured to the mystery and excitement of doing something taboo. However, I was not looking to have an affair.

MT: How long did you know this woman before you were involved with her intimately?

CB: Just three months. Her husband went out of town on a weeknight. My wife had a small group meeting to go to. "Kate" asked me if I wanted to grab a cup of coffee after work, so I did. And things progressed from there.

MT: You had sex with her.

CB: Yes.

MT: Did you both feel guilty afterward?

CB: Oh, it was horrible. The next day at the office, "Kate" wouldn't even look at me. And to be honest, I didn't feel the need to look at her either.

MT: What happened next?

CB: About two days later, we finally talked about it. We apologized to each other and made a promise that it would never happen again. But deep down inside, I think we both wanted it to happen again. There was an excitement to this that became addictive. We ended up having sex again about a week later. This went on for nearly eight months.

Matthew, it was like I was playing a game. I had never experienced anything so tempting in all my life. As much as I didn't want to hurt my wife, I didn't want this to end either.

MT: What were you saying to God at this time?

CB: Every time something happened, I would tell God it would never happen again. I'd hear a sermon that would cause me

91

to feel incredibly guilty, and I would make another empty promise to him. It was like I was living two different lives.

MT: How did it finally come to an end?

CB: Our co-worker had been suspecting that something was going on the entire time. He finally reported us to the church's leadership. When "Kate" was confronted, she confessed. I tried to hide, to lie my way out of it for a while, until the pastor told me that "Kate" had already told him the truth. We both lost our jobs.

MT: What did you tell your wife?

CB: Well, first I called my pastor and asked him if I could meet with him. I told him the whole story. And I asked if he would be there with me when I told my wife. He said that he would.

MT: Obviously, your wife was devastated.

CB: I can hardly put into words what I witnessed. You would have thought she had just found me dead on the street . . . I could hear her heart aching.

MT: Cameron, what did she say to you?

CB: She called me every name in the book. To be honest, I'd rather not discuss what she said to me.

MT: Tell me what happened after this.

CB: At first, my wife went to stay with her parents. She moved out of our home and filed for divorce a little more than a month later. I tried to apologize. I tried to find the right words to say. But *my* heart was in such a horrible place during this time that I couldn't even begin to know how to reconcile everything. I ended up taking six months off from work. I went to counseling. I started going to a different church.

MT: I know that you're still hurting, but can you describe for me what's going on in your heart now?

CB: I've been silenced. I never expected my life to be this way. I imagined being married to my wife forever. I wanted three kids. I planned on us growing old together. I've been humbled. And when you're humbled, there are very few words one can say that even begin to make sense.

MT: What about your faith—where are you spiritually?

CB: I'm not exactly sure. I know where I want to be. I want to be resting in the grace of Christ. I want to know that God has forgiven me—that he still wants me as his child. But I'm not there yet. I don't believe I will be there for a long time.

Update: Cameron found a church that was willing to hire him on to do design work. Although he still misses being married, he is learning to be content with the consequences of his mistakes.

6

joy is a lifestyle

In 1989, the Berlin Wall began to crumble. With pickaxes and hammers, East Germans began bombarding that wall with anything they could find. Nearly thirty years after its construction in 1961, the tearing down of that wall of oppression and control was the defining sign of the end of the Cold War. I watched in awe as the pictures were beamed from East Germany to television sets around the world. Thousands upon thousands of people joined in the celebration. People who had never experienced freedom and liberty went running and shouting through the streets with visible joy on their faces and audible joy on their lips. One couldn't help but get goose bumps just watching their experience. Seeing their utter elation made you want to join in. I even remember feeling just a little bit jealous.

It's a little ridiculous, but as a sixteen-year-old kid, I had never seen that kind of joy before.

My grandmother always said that joy is contagious. She was right. As a kid, I liked being around joyful people, but I don't remember knowing too many. Of course, I knew people who laughed a lot and told hilariously funny stories, but even then I knew that wasn't necessarily joy. To me, the people who didn't know Jesus seemed to be more joyful than those who did know him. The "sinners," as my church always called them, seemed to be freer and more stable than those who frequented my church. They laughed more heartily and lived more passionately than the religious dads and moms I knew. So for me, as a kid growing up in very religious surroundings, joy was an elusive quality that very few enjoyed.

However, when I encountered true joy, I knew it. My grandmother, or "Mammom," as we called her, was joyful. Whenever she walked into a room, her sweet smile and the pure love of life came with her. There was a wise and relentless contentment to her that people liked being around. I've always wanted to emulate the actions of my grandmother because her joy seemed so authentic and so true.

Kids have always been a big reminder of joy to me. As a twenty-four-year-old idealist just out of business school with my bachelor of business administration from Belmont University, I knew that my first priority was to find a good-paying job. Unfortunately, that task proved to be much harder than I expected. During the hunt to find my true employment calling, I worked a few part-time jobs to "make ends meet." One of those "in-between" jobs was a stint as a substitute teacher for the Kent County Board of Education in Chestertown, Maryland. I was surprised at the state of Maryland's willingness to let anyone with a high school education, a clean record, and a loving heart fill in for their finest teachers. Even more startling was the fact that they let a young punk like myself stand in as one of those molders of young minds.

One of my favorite "teaching" experiences was at the state's top-rated Millington Elementary School, where a bunch of first graders taught me much more than I ever could have taught them. One of the first things I learned about first graders is their honesty. They are *thoroughly* honest. They'll say out loud just about anything that jets through their young brains. One youngster named Alex told me one morning that my breath was so bad he didn't want to talk to me anymore. It's unbelievable how much impact a six-year-old can have on your self-esteem; you can bet that was the last time I walked into that school without a healthy supply of Altoids. But even more than their sometimes embarrassingly blatant honesty, the thing that stuck with me about those kids was their sheer joy for life.

The kids at Millington Elementary School laughed big and loud and often. They passionately pursued everything. I could stand in front of the class and act like a complete idiot, and they *still* thought I was cool and inspiring. It didn't matter if we were in the classroom, on the playground, in the hallways, or taking a spelling test, these kids had joyful spirits that radiated through their smiles, laughs, and facial expressions. Joy was a part of their lifestyle. They seemed to have this undying desire to make everything they encountered fun, exciting, and engaging. Of course, it's not like they knew they were doing it. But that made their joy even more intriguing. It wasn't forced or pretended; they weren't consciously pursuing joy—it was just a part of who they were as people. All of us could use a little lesson in joy from that classroom of six-year-olds.

During my term as a substitute, I had the opportunity to teach a week or two in every grade. I sat in kindergarten classes, I sat in fifth-grade gym classes, and I sat in senior English classes. And it was astonishing for me to observe firsthand the joy that humanity loses in twelve short years. The experience left me befuddled. The most backward and difficult six-year-old kid in Mrs. Franton's first grade class was more confident, joyful, and self-assured than the most outgoing senior in the English class. While those six-year-olds were confident and happy, the seniors were quiet and awkward and seemed to lack the basic strengths that come from knowing joy.

What happens between those very crucial years of six and seventeen that steals away joy? Yes, I know puberty happens. And I know somewhere around fourth or fifth grade kids begin realizing they're not as pretty or skinny or smart as another kid. And I understand that a lot of life (sometimes horrible life) can happen during those years—parents divorce, friends commit suicide, you experiment with drugs, you lose your innocence, you question your sexuality, you are ridiculed and hated by peers. I've seen and experienced how the pain and insecurities in life can steal joy from so many people from all walks of life.

But still, despite my limited experiences of knowing people who truly understood joy, my faith has led me to believe wholeheartedly in the power of joy and its immense ability to bring about a miracle in the human soul. And I'm not simply referring to the joy that a six-year-old exudes on the playground or the joy that radiates from the face of a man who has just tasted freedom for the first time, but a joy that comes from a change within, a joy that begins with a life of faith in a joyful God.

Humanity has a constant need for joy. It's programmed inside of us to look for something that makes us *feel* joyful. I believe that God has put inside all of us the need for utter pleasure, contentment, and happiness. And you don't have to look very hard at culture to see that people invest a great deal of time, money, and self in pursuit of such feelings.

Many Christians believe that any joy brought on by sinful or selfish means is not joy at all. I have to disagree. The world certainly has some grandiose impersonations of true joy. I do not believe that joy gained from selfish behavior is pure joy or lasting joy, but it does often bring instantaneous pleasure and happiness that do a good job at masquerading as joy. If what the world offers to us on a regular basis didn't at least bring some version of joy, how then would you explain its mass appeal?

One of my old neighbors frequently visits nude bars for personal pleasure. He's invited me several times to go with him. I've always declined gracefully. But still, Jim swears that a lap dance from a mostly naked woman makes him feel joyous and alive. I'm sure many men would agree that there's a certain joy in even the thought. We Christians are quick to respond to a nude bar attendee with, "That's not *real* joy." But a non-Christian is not going to comprehend what he is unable to see. If a man believes this habit indeed brings him a feeling not unlike joy, it's hard for a Christian to come along and refute that belief.

I believe that an individual's belief system plays a major role in what defines "pure joy" in that person's life. If a person believes they can find joy in X, then that individual will do whatever necessary to experience X, live with X, partake in X. It's not unlike mathematics. If X plus Y equals *JOY*, then many of us find the quickest and easiest way to get X and Y together.

Back in 1995, I went to the theatre and watched the third installment to the Batman series, *Batman Forever*, starring Val Kilmer and Jim Carrey. Carrey played the ever-mischievous Riddler, and he was very convincing as the man with all the riddles and rhymes. One scene that entertained me was when the Riddler suddenly became overwhelmed with a purely evil thought. He shivered in ecstasy (as only Jim Carrey can) and said to himself, "Aaaahhhh, joygasm!" And as silly as it is, that odd combination of words explains a lot about the kind of joy that people today are seeking. Instead of looking for pure joy, people want a good, satisfying joygasm. We want the quick fix. And that is exactly what the enemy is selling.

The evil one is all about selling joy "quickies." Satan's ability to manipulate us into thinking we're getting a "good buy" is not really that uncanny. He's always prided himself in offering people substitutes for truth. And as we see in our modern culture, Satan's supply of *joygasmic* experiences sells out fast. And while I've spent a great deal of time harping on the non-Christian's tendency to buy into the subtleties of Satan's salesmanship, we Christians are buying too. We buy in bulk. We don't go to the "store" every other day; instead we buy false joy in large quantities because we don't want to be seen making such purchases. So, we stock up.

It's no secret that people of faith struggle to understand where lasting joy comes from. So many of us look for joy in all the wrong places. We expect church to be our source of lasting joy. We hope that our families will bring us lasting joy. We want our good health, great marriages, and influential jobs to bring us lasting joy. We are quick to proclaim that we know joy comes from our faith in Jesus, but our lives all too often fail to reflect that belief.

Some in the church would have us believe that you must be happy and charismatic all of the time to be considered joyful. *Those* people don't understand joy, at least not the contagious, God-experience joy I have come to strive for. I call it "lifestyle joy."

The apostle Paul shouted from the rooftops that the joy of the Lord is our strength. He said that the only kind of joy that will strengthen us is the kind of joy that comes from a relationship with Jesus. He also said that joy was one of the fruits of the Spirit—that a person relying on the "transforming power" of Jesus's blood will give birth to a godly joy.

I want that kind of joy. I'm tired of my life being inundated with negativity and cynicism. If the joy of the Lord is our strength, then I must admit that I have so often been very weak.

Most God-followers know that joy is not found in anything this world has to offer. Of course, society is constantly telling us otherwise. We are constantly misled to believe that lifestyle joy can be attained by our own means. Some Christians think that joy comes if you pray harder or read Scripture more. And certainly those are great habits, but lifestyle joy isn't something we can work toward; it's an existence we live.

There was a time in my life when I was so overcome with bitterness and anger toward the church that it was impossible for me to live a life of joy. In fact, joy was one of the first things to go. So I tried to find joy elsewhere.

I often compare my own story to the story in Exodus about the Hebrew children wandering in the wilderness with Moses for forty years. Poor Moses; it was just about impossible for him to make those people happy. When they needed water, God provided. When they needed food, God gave manna from heaven. When they needed a guide, he was a cloud by day and a ball of fire by night. I often thought while reading this story, *What were these people looking for?* Not only did the Israelites have their daily concerns handled for them, they had God as their personal tour guide. He proved to them again and again that he was with them. And still they complained, became bitter, and eventually sought out other things to worship. The Hebrew children were obviously looking for joy in their circumstances, and when their fulfilled circumstances didn't make them feel good, they turned to other means to find joy. They tried complaining. They tried looking for their own way through the wilderness. Until one day Moses came back from one of his conversations with God and found the same people who had once worshiped God with abandon were dancing around and worshiping a golden calf—just like the rest of the world.

I can personally understand the predicament of the Hebrew children. Many times in my own life I have sought out joy in the most disgusting of places. I've found a few elements of joy in greed, materialism, cynicism, and porn. When you're desperate, you'll go to any means necessary to just *feel* alive. You hope that something will prove to be an outlet of investment where you can find something satisfying. And many times I did find some satisfaction. If I was lonely or feeling selfish—it didn't matter—a quick fix of my own kind of joy did the trick.

The Hebrew children believed too that joy and satisfaction would be found in something other than God's faithfulness. And for a moment, because of their flawed belief system, they found what they were looking for. Did they find *real* joy? Well, they thought they had.

But it's in these types of situations where one's faith intervenes.

With our belief systems so intertwined with our own personal opinions of what defines true joy, God comes into the lives of his children and breaks down our flawed beliefs and rebuilds the structure of truth. We cannot begin to comprehend God's lifestyle of joy without truth; it's spiritually inconceivable. That's not to say you're not experiencing a type of joy living your life outside of his grace, mercy, and justice; you're just not experiencing *his* joy. And as those desiring to know a loving Father, his joy should be our passion.

I've learned through my own God-experience that it takes great faith to live a life of joy. It's not just a feeling you decide to put on in the morning; it takes a change in lifestyle to experience it. Joy comes through submission to the ways of the Father. Joy comes through humbling oneself to the altering Spirit of God's work in one's daily life. Joy is the symptom of a life surrendered to the will of Jesus.

I love King David. I love him because I am able to so closely relate to him and his longing to know God. He was *very* human, which is beautifully apparent in his passion and his struggle to be intimate with the Almighty. There are times when I read Scripture and think that King David sinned almost as passionately as he praised. He was a poet, a lover, a warrior, an adulterer, and a feeler. But my favorite quality of David was his extreme passion to know joy.

In Psalm 9:2, one of the many references to joy in the Psalms, King David cried out, "I will be filled with joy because of you" (NLT). David knew the secret. It was no mystery to him, the nearness of joy. He knew it was found in pursuing the Father. His life was far from perfect, and he certainly had his moments where he sought out joy through other means, but still David's faith kept leading him back to the pure joy of God. Even in the midst of trial and judgment, David found joy in confession and worship.

When I met Cynthia Warren via an email she sent to me regarding something I had written about my battle with depression, she seemed depressed herself—very depressed. Her husband had an affair two years prior to our meeting.

Without therapy or any chance of recovery, she divorced him. She told me in her email that he was "an obnoxious, arrogant prick." She went on to write that even though she had done nothing wrong, she felt guilty and had lost her ability to even see the possibility of joy coming out of a situation like this.

A Christian, Cynthia was active in church, taught a fifth-grade girls' Sunday school class, and sang in the choir. She was surrounded by people, but she kept her depression a secret from everyone—even her family.

I wrote Cynthia back a few days later. Hesitantly, I told her that it sounded like she needed to seek out therapy right away. I told her that I would pray for her.

Weeks went by, and Cynthia wrote me again.

"I went to see my pastor," she wrote. "It was good to finally be able to verbalize some of my feelings. You were right; I am depressed. I've actually scheduled an appointment to see a Christian therapist next week. But what I still can't comprehend is how God is going to bring joy, peace, and comfort out of a situation like this . . ."

Like so many of us, Cynthia was looking for God to bring joy out of her painful circumstance. This is flawed thinking. Painful situations suck. God doesn't magically allow us to find joy during bad times. Cynthia was seemingly expecting that God would suddenly reveal why her husband had an affair and that somehow she would feel joy because of God's explanation. Unfortunately, we might never know why God allows certain painful situations to happen to us. Even though Cynthia knew that God was the provider of lifestyle joy, she was focused on her situation to get her there. But joy is *not* found in making sense of our situations. Joy is found in knowing God, and it's sustained through our faith in him.

Ultimately, we experience lifestyle joy when we become content with who Jesus is. Jesus said, "I am the way, the truth, and the life. No one can come to the Father except through me" (John 14:6 NLT). Making peace with this statement is a process. Some days I wake up and am completely fine with Jesus being the "way" or the "truth" for me. But then there are times when I'm not okay with his way or truth; I want it to be my way or I want to find my *own* truth. But my rules and my idols and my belief systems only get in the way of Jesus reigning supreme in my life. Joy comes not when we put Jesus first, but when we realize that he's always been first and demands nothing less. We must get ourselves out of the way in order for his purpose of making us like him to transpire.

We will never find our joy in circumstance. We will never find our joy in the "quickies" culture so often offers. Joy comes to us when we faithfully pursue knowing Jesus more intimately. As you begin to know him more deeply and more passionately, you will see your life becoming more peaceful, more content. You won't be "happy all the time," but your joy will be a lifestyle and not just a passing feeling.

7

know Jesus; know him well

George Bashner is a missionary in Indonesia where great violence against Christians is common. The village where he lives is home to thousands of common folk who have never heard the gospel of Jesus. Much like Jennifer Garner's character on *Alias*, Bashner's ministry work is undercover. He can't tell me much about his daily duties, his actual location, or his accomplishments without putting his family in grave danger. When you ask him what he does for a living, he replies, "I am a teacher"—which isn't exactly a lie; he does volunteer to teach English at a local children's school in the village where he lives. But Bashner's calling isn't teaching Indonesian children their *ABC*s; his mission is purely evangelical.

Every morning Bashner wakes up while it is still dark outside, walks down to the nearby Indian Ocean, sits on the ground, and puts his face to the sand. Sometimes there's a soft mist of ocean water hitting him in the face as the waves come crashing in. Other times the ocean is as crystal clear as a sheet of glass. It is here, in this place, in this position, that Bashner talks out loud to Jesus. You see, Jesus and he are close. They have to be. Because if George wasn't in love with Jesus, he would not be living below poverty level in a world where violence thrives—and consequently, he wouldn't be having the time of his life.

"When I turned thirty-four, Jesus called me to be a missionary," Bashner told me. "Telling my wife I felt called to do this was difficult. But she told me she trusted my relationship with Jesus enough to know that he would not lead us astray. . . . It's been seven years since that conversation, and Jesus and I have only gotten closer.

"In order for me to really hear Jesus and trust his words, I had to get to know him like I had never known him before."

How did that happen, George?

"Well, at age twenty-two I began studying the life of Christ on my own. It wasn't a part of any Bible study or church function. I just wanted to really know him, so I began rereading his words, memorizing his deeds, and asking him to speak to me."

What was your greatest "Aha" moment during that time?

"When Jesus walked on water, Peter jumped out of the boat to join him. My 'Aha' moment was when I realized that I was called to be one of those who jumped out of the boat. I know this from spending time with Jesus and getting to know his heart for me. Not everyone can be like Peter, but I know I was called to it."

Have you ever fallen in the water and had to have Jesus walk you back to the boat?

[He laughs.] "All the time. But I've learned so much during those times of getting out of the boat, that the moments of humility, when I again realize I can't do it on my own, are sweet and so very needed.

"I had to know God before I could trust him."

Human beings cannot trust God, have faith in him, or find joy in him without knowing him—intimately and personally. We need to know his personality. We need to know what his passions are. We need to know what he hates, what he loves, and what makes him giddy with pride. But most importantly, we need to know what he wants for us as individuals. Only when we know him can we trust him to be good, faithful, and just.

Many people, all over the world, claim to know God but still do not trust him. Trusting God is contingent on us knowing him. Our knowledge of who he is translates into us being changed. But too often people are scared of change. We resist it. In fact, many of us resist knowing God because knowing him leads to listening to him, and when we listen to God, our humanity is diminished and the life of God is illuminated in us.

But that's right where we need to be. Provocative faith requires that we only value the light and authority of God—that we get out of his way so he can make us into what he wants us to be. Is this hard? It's amazingly difficult to put yourself last, to put your ideals and opinions on the "back burner." But as we get to know Jesus—his likes and passions and mysteries—we begin to pursue becoming more like him.

After God woke me up to the fact that I had been abusing our relationship (see chapter 1), I realized that I needed to reidentify myself with Christ, get to know him intimately, and understand his heart. So I began reacquainting myself with Jesus.

My quest to know Jesus began with a personal study of the Sermon on the Mount (Matthew 5–7). Jesus talks fervently about his own heart and his heart for us in this sermon. In these three chapters of Scripture, we find out things about Jesus that are imperative for his followers to know. We learn about his sincere love for the poor, how he prayed to his Father, and how he abhorred murder and adultery. But, maybe most importantly, we learn much about his personality.

Jesus's words here were controversial and blunt, yet gentle and commanding. He was eloquent but personable. Why do you think Jesus's audience later questioned, "Who is this man who speaks with such authority?" They no doubt found Jesus to be a strange and beautiful contradiction to the religious message their ears had become accustomed to hearing. However, his message wasn't contradictory; on the contrary, it was fulfilling everything these people had heard many times before.

Unfortunately, many of the people during Jesus's times failed to understand his words; they failed to truly hear him and know him in the way Jesus so desired for them to.

Today, Jesus has the same request for us. He wants us to know him.

When I began this quest to know Jesus, I was many times surprised by what I learned. I was shocked when the words of Christ refuted several teachings that I had been taught to believe for so long. These were teachings my church believed in wholeheartedly.

I was taught most of my life to be a separatist. I was led to believe that not only should my actions be anticultural, righteous, and incorruptible, but that I should not associate myself with people who believe differently than I do. I was told that hanging out with "sinners" would lead me astray. An analogy the preacher from my church often used was that of a fruit basket piled high with lush, ripe apples. If one bad apple were left in the basket, the good apples would not make the bad apple ripe and eatable. No! The bad apple would eventually make the good apples bad. This is a true statement but a ridiculous analogy. You can't compare humans, who are in need of redemptive grace in order to be made "good," to a basket full of good, ripe apples. Yet sadly, this teaching kept me from associating myself with "sinners" for most of my life.

In getting to know Jesus through Scripture, I realized that he actually hung out with the sinners, prostitutes, and tax collectors. I never got the chance to talk with that preacher about his unfortunate "bad apple" example, but it would probably be pointless anyway. I don't think that preacher would hang with someone like me.

One morning when I was sixteen years old, I woke up to an empty house. It was quiet and still. At first, I felt somewhat awkward. I wasn't used to waking up to such quiet. The TV and the radio weren't on. I didn't hear the footsteps of my mother stirring in the kitchen. The shower wasn't running. No one was talking too loudly. And although I wasn't accustomed to such a sterile morning routine—I really liked it this way.

I hadn't been abandoned. My parents had simply left town for a weekend vacation to Amish country in Lancaster, Pennsylvania. I opted out of the trip to the German world of horse and buggies when my father deemed me old enough to stay home alone. I hadn't stayed home alone before—at least, not for any length of time—so I was looking forward to my first time alone.

Of course, to my sixteen-year-old brain, being alone in a big house for three days spelled only one thing: freedom—and lots of it. I longed for the kind of freedom that caused an unexplained excitement to well up inside when the rules and expectations of your parents are temporarily gone. And for the first time, you get to breathe deep breaths of life on your own. I had my weekend all planned out.

For three glorious days, I would take full reign of my parents' house. So what did I want to do? I wanted to live my idea of a king's life. I wanted to watch TV until 2 a.m. I wanted to walk around the house naked and free. I wanted to have friends over to cook burgers and hot dogs on the grill. I wanted to eat half a container of Breyer's vanilla bean ice cream. And that was just my list for the first day! But sadly, none of that happened.

Finding a little human freedom proved difficult because Jesus decided he would come for a visit to see me. Okay, so he didn't knock on the front door and welcome himself in for a cup of coffee. No, it wasn't like that at all.

Two o'clock in the morning came around, and I was up watching old *I Love Lucy* reruns. I was restless; to tell the truth, I was a little bit scared in the empty, lonely house. I wanted to go sleep, but it just wasn't happening. And my love for old black-and-white comedies was growing stale. But that's when I heard him.

"Worship me."

It's rather hard to explain to the everyday person about the concept of God speaking. It wasn't necessarily audible, but I heard it nonetheless. I ignored it at first. I thought it was me talking to myself. But then I heard it again.

"Worship me. Get down on your face and worship me."

I had to respond. There wasn't a choice. So I moved from the couch and sat in the middle of my living room floor and began to listen. And listening, for me, was a big step. Listening to that "still, small voice of God" is hard work for many people, but for me it's sometimes darn near impossible.

But on that particular morning, I couldn't help but respond to the presence of Jesus Christ. For the first time in my life, I *heard* Jesus speak.

I began worshiping him with song, prayer, silence, dance, and journaling. Here's an excerpt from what I wrote in my journal:

> I'm in awe of you, God. I can't see you, but I know you're here with me. Forgive me if I don't have the right words to say. I've never experienced something like this before. And for a moment, I was scared of you. But now, I see that you're wanting me to listen. Help me listen. Help me hear you. Help me to know your voice.

113

Today, I hear God's voice. That prayer I wrote when I was sixteen years old has been answered. I know my Father's voice. But we can't know him without listening.

I used to laugh at Dorothy Hinson when she would tell me stories about her interactions with God. The large, forty-something woman would walk into the Christian bookstore where I worked and tell me unbelievable experiences about what God had accomplished in her life. I laughed because, from my spiritually naïve point of view, her stories were more than a little strange. In fact, I thought some of them were downright ridiculous. You see, Dorothy went to the more charismatic church in town. One time she claimed that the Spirit of God moved so freely in her church that the entire congregation began waddling around like ducks, flapping their arms like they were wings, and making "tweet" and "quack" noises with their lips. I had never heard anything so bizarre in all my life. At the time, I didn't know whether to laugh or perform an exorcism.

There are God-followers like Dorothy all over the world. Some more conservative Christians might think Dorothy is misguided or uninformed, or even pagan. But I'm often reminded about the character of God through people like Dorothy. If I can believe that God used an individual like John the Baptist to be a forerunner for his Son, then I can believe God passionately interacts with a crazy loon like Dorothy.

Miss Dorothy's life ended with a losing battle to cancer. I am told her spirit never once whimpered about the pain, the circumstance, or the untimely occurrence of her death. In fact, instead of complaining or fearing, Dorothy would tell the nurses about Jesus, tell her close friends more "crazy stories," and go around encouraging the other cancer patients at the hospital. How was she able to do this? I am convinced Dorothy Hinson knew Jesus and knew him well. People's skepticism about her uncanny faith in God didn't cause her to waver. In fact, it didn't even occur to her that she was the least bit crazy. Her passion was Jesus.

After finishing my degree, I began waiting tables. The idea of working as a server right out of college was not really my ideal first step toward my future career, but it was what was available at the time. About five months into my job, I became convinced that God was calling me to go to seminary. Naturally, I hightailed it home to pursue furthering my education. When I got there, I expected God to make everything easy. I thought that since he had called me to this, he would pave the way for me to go. But instead of it being easy for me to go to seminary, it was impossible. Every single possible door slammed shut in my face.

At the age of twenty-four, I found myself living with my parents and working a factory job for $6.50 an hour. I hated it. I hated it so much that I thought I had heard God wrong. I thought maybe I should return to Nashville and go back to serving tables. I packed my car and planned to go back as quickly as I came home. The night before I left, God said to me in no uncertain terms, "Do not go back to Nashville." Thus began an argument between God and me: *What?!? God, you move me eight hundred miles away from my friends, the music business, and a paying job to what—a dead-end job making a little above minimum wage? That's not my idea of you working things out. You closed the seminary door in my face; what am I supposed to do?*

To say that I was frustrated with God would be a huge understatement. A pastor friend told me to stop and listen intently to what God was saying to me and trust his words. The night before I was to leave, I told my parents that I could not return to Nashville. Instead, I went back to that dead-end job, working beside colleagues who didn't even have high school educations—in fact, some of them barely had teeth.

I spent the next fourteen months listening for God's voice. I frequently put words in his mouth. I thought he wanted me to be a teacher, so I looked into pursuing my teaching certification. That door closed too. My father encouraged me to apply for a job at the financial institution MBNA. I did, and I was offered the job. But I turned it down because this time I felt that God was saying, "No, this is not for you." My father and I had a huge argument over me turning this job down, but I told Dad that I knew this was not what God wanted me to do. Fortunately for me, he respected that.

Fourteen months after I had decided to move home, a friend whom I met through that dead-end job introduced me to her close entrepreneurial friend, who also happened to be a wealthy and influential philanthropist. We chatted by phone on a Sunday afternoon. By the following Sunday I had been offered my dream job. This friend of a friend offered me a job as the manager of a faith-based coffeehouse. And this time, God said clearly and enthusiastically, "Yes! This is your calling!" If I had not taken that position, I honestly believe I would not be here writing this book.

If I hadn't known Jesus, his voice, his expectation of me, I would have settled for a life he didn't want me to live. When we pursue knowing Jesus—not just through church, youth group, or Bible study—but through our own study of Scripture, meditation, and intimacy, we are yielding our lives to him.

I meditate. Unfortunately, I don't meditate as often as I know I should. A beautiful thing happens when I meditate. The world gets shut out, and for a few short moments I am alone with my Savior, thinking only of him.

I'm sure I look silly sprawled out in the middle of my living room floor, wearing nothing but a pair of boxer briefs and a T-shirt, with candles lit all around me. But this is where my faith is restored. This is where I hear Jesus speak my name. I trust more because I meditate. I have more joy because I meditate. I hear God because I meditate. The Bible commands us to meditate on God's Word day and night—so that's what I do. In the quietness of my house, Jesus meets me, and I set my mind on him.

If you get one thing from this book, let it be this: meditation on Jesus will change your spiritual life. It will rejuvenate your faith like nothing else you will ever experience. More than a great sermon, more than listening to a radio teaching, more than reading this book, meditation on Christ—what he did, who he is, and what he wants of you—will give your life focus, and it will make your faith provocative. And you will begin to know him like never before.

Young singer gets REAL honest with God

I met singer/songwriter Kendall Payne when she came to perform at Jammin' Java in 1999. We became friends. Since then, I have watched her career move from the grand echelons of radio and movie soundtrack success to once again becoming a struggling musician having a hard time scraping enough money together to make a new album. Kendall has never been one to shy away from speaking the truth. And in my interview with her, she is no different.

MT: Kendall, you've had a dream to perform your music for quite some time. How has God altered this dream over the years?

KP: Well, for starters he's demolished it. It seems to me that I started out with best of intentions, but totally unaware of my own heart. Which I don't believe God faults me for. My heart was concerned with self-promotion, even though I could not see it at that time. I truly believed my dream was honoring to God—and I was mostly unaware of how honoring it was to my own ego and sense of self.

MT: How did you respond to his alterations? What did you feel?

KP: At first I faked it, believing that God was "testing" me. I pretended not to falter in my faith, but that only lasts so long. Inevitably we had it out! I was utterly disappointed with him. I felt like he had failed me. I could not see the person who would eventually emerge on the other side of this tunnel of darkness and disappointment.

MT: Tell me about the last time you were angry with God over his involvement or seeming uninvolvement in your life.

KP: I remember lying in bed one night, feeling so alone, finally turning my face to the ceiling and saying out loud, "*You! You* did this to me! *You* have broken my heart!" Where do you turn when the shelter and safe place is the eye of the storm? You have no choice but to lean into the storm and let it strip away all that you used as security. I felt like he set me up to fail. He was supposed to be my comfort—not the reason I felt distressed. God calls himself an "ever-present help in times of trouble," but during that particular time he felt like the eye of the storm.

MT: Does he talk back?

KP: Oh yeah! But he *never* says what I want him to. And he *never* explains himself. What I hear when he speaks to me is "Oh my precious one, I am not finished with you yet." Which reassures me I am dear to him. I need nothing else.

MT: God has taken you from having a major-label release to an independent release, from having many people working around you to you doing most of the work yourself. How would you describe the journey?

KP: I believe wholeheartedly that the journey *is* the destination. I used to think "arriving" was the most important part. Now I see that every step along the way is as crucial and significant as the final step, which normally gets all the credit and press. I consider each seemingly uneventful and other times overwhelmingly busy day incredibly important—teaching a profound lesson that the tomorrows and yesterdays could not unravel for me. So it doesn't matter much anymore if I'm with a major label or going the indie route. I welcome any and all new experiences—and only ask that God grow me up through them.

MT: What have you learned about faith in this journey?

KP: In my past I regurgitated half-truths, clichéd truths, and even well-intentioned truths, yet they have served as nothing more than a Band-Aid neatly placed on a cancer-ridden body. Each has failed in its oversimplified form to answer life's deepest and darkest questions. My faith is no longer in the God I believe in (*me* and *my belief* being the most important part of the equation)—my faith rests solidly now in the God who *is* (regardless of whether I understand him). And maybe a better way to say it has already been said: "And so you see I have come to doubt all that I once held as true. I stand alone without beliefs the only truth I know is You" [Paul Simon, "Kathy's Song"].

119

8

love relentlessly

I've written about Devon before. He's a man whose story I read about many years ago online in one of those diary-type websites. His story was a sad portrayal of where sin can leave an individual. Devon was a twenty-six-year-old troubled soul working as a male prostitute in the downtown business district of Miami. He made nearly three thousand a week "servicing" high-profile businessmen and women whom he met in chat rooms online.

It had been his goal to escape his illegal employment by moving away from his hometown of Washington DC to the southeast coast of Florida. He hoped to make a new start, but a drug habit and the need to make some quick cash lured him back into his controversial trade.

Devon's story included big, fancy parties where he was paid top dollar to "perform," interactions with C- and D-level celebrities who would buy him nice clothes and good cocaine, and the occasional meeting with politicians who paid mostly for his willingness to keep quiet. After almost two years of living this life, Devon became depressed and suicidal, and he started seeking support.

Devon visited a church in South Florida, hoping to find a life that was real and authentic. He liked the church. He ended up joining a Bible study, and six months into his time at this church, he broke down in front of the group of six men and shared his story. Two of the men were completely freaked out by the details of Devon's life. They refused to be a part of a Bible study with someone of his background. The pastor of the church tried to intervene, but news of Devon's story traveled quickly around the church. Feeling even more defeated, Devon left the church.

Unfortunately, nearly two years after visiting that church, Devon's life ended tragically in an apparent suicide. No one knows for sure, but it seems unlikely that he ever found the love he was looking for. At least, he didn't find it in this lifetime.

Stories like Devon's can be found all across the globe and in nearly every type of community. People whose lives are devastated by sin, confusion, and hopelessness end up turning to the church for acceptance and love, but instead they find judgment, fear, and resistance. I've seen this behavior firsthand over and over again in the churches I have visited. This is why I am thoroughly convinced that individuals with a desire to pursue provocative faith must learn to love—with no strings attached. Now, it's not that there aren't *any* churches that love with no strings attached—just too few of them.

On October 31, 1999, Jesus came to me with a request at 2:36 a.m.

Over the past twenty-seven years of following him, if there is one thing I've learned about Jesus, it's that he has no sense of earthly timing. His schedule is not like mine. He'll come to us at any time to teach us, give us advice, talk to us, or love on us.

This time I was sleeping on a friend's couch in Nashville, Tennessee, when Jesus woke me up rather abruptly with a particular Scripture he wanted me to read. It startled me a little. But instead of ignoring the nudge and going back to sleep, I reached for my Bible, which was sitting on top of my suitcase a few feet away, and quickly turned to the Scripture reference: "Love the Lord your God with all your heart, all your soul, all your strength, and all your mind. And love your neighbor as yourself" (Luke 10:27 NLT).

Seriously, a part of me was like, *You woke me up for this?* I knew this verse by heart. I had read this verse a thousand times before. Jesus called the two sentences of this verse the two greatest of all the commandments. Hundreds of sermons have been preached on them. They have been turned into too many songs to count. In other words, they were *very* familiar. I'll be honest; I was a little disappointed with the "message."

Not knowing what Jesus wanted me to learn, I sat up in my bed and said a simple prayer asking God to reveal what he wanted me to learn from these words. And in no uncertain terms, he asked me to relearn how to love him and the people around me. Being somewhat paranoid about being questioned, a dialogue began running through my head.

What? I already love you, Jesus. You know I love you. Sure, I probably don't show it the way I should, but that doesn't mean I don't love you. Does it? It shouldn't. Because I do.

Jesus was adamant. He began to remind me of my actions. My heart began to break at the thought of the many lives I had hurt because of my lack of love for people. Not to mention what Jesus must have thought about my lack of love for him.

Over the next couple of weeks, I found through studying Scripture that Jesus talked a lot about loving him and loving the Father. In John 14:21 he said, "Those who obey my commandments are the ones who love me. And because they love me, my Father will love them, and I will love them. And I will reveal myself to each one of them" (NLT). In Matthew 10:37, Jesus was even more definitive when he said, "If you love your father or mother more than you love me, you are not worthy of being mine; or if you love your son or daughter more than me, you are not worthy of being mine" (NLT). Obviously, Jesus believed that the strongest human love known existed between a parent and a child, but he made it quite clear that this love cannot compare to the love he expects from us. I have heard it said that our love for Jesus is a measuring stick of sorts for our priorities, what we value, and what comes first in our lives. If our priorities are out of whack, then usually our love for him is too. When we are fully in love with Jesus, nothing else matters but serving him and his kingdom.

The verse Jesus revealed to me at 2:30 in the morning on Halloween 1999 is found in Matthew 22:37, Mark 12:30, and again in Luke 10:27. The commandments to love God and love our neighbor are cited in three of the four Gospels, underscoring their importance. The two are interchangeable. We can't love Jesus without loving other people. And we can't love people without first loving Jesus.

In other words, love people with all of your heart and you will be loving Jesus; love Jesus with all of your heart and you will be loving people. *That's the only "measuring stick" you need.* It was quite obvious to me that I fell far short of God's expectation of me to love.

Dennis Kirkland loves teenagers more than any man I have ever known. He is a short man with a big personality. Kids are drawn to his humor, New York dialect, and his crazy love of life. As a career youth minister, he had worked at several different churches and had seen God work miracles in the lives of troubled kids at each and every location. Simply put, Dennis is a gifted individual. I had the pleasure of volunteering for Dennis at one of the churches where he worked for five years.

Although I had worked with teenagers before at a couple smaller churches and with one parachurch organization, I was still rough and awkward around teenagers. I didn't necessarily have the greatest teen experience myself (not hitting puberty until I was nearly eighteen years old certainly didn't help). But I got to know Dennis while working at Jammin' Java, the faith-based coffeehouse, and I thought it would be very interesting to do ministry beside him.

After every youth meeting, Dennis and the rest of us youth leaders got together for Heineken and American-made cigars. It was our way of calming down after an energetic day of ministry. Much emotion went into working with young people, and this was a time when we could debrief and discuss how we could do things better. I learned a lot about loving people from these conversations. But in one instance in particular, it got personal.

"Matthew," said Dennis late one Sunday night while puffing away on his stogie, "you were much too hard on those two young men tonight."

I looked at him somewhat shocked, as if to say, "*Me?*"

"You're too tense, bro. You've got to loosen up, or you'll never see God use you the way you desire."

"I need to loosen up?" I asked bluntly. I thought for sure I was too loose now. I was far away from my days at the church of my childhood, where it would have been a sin to even breathe in the secondhand smoke of a cigar.

"You're too consumed with how the kids are dressed, behaving, the words they are using—when you should be much more concerned for their hearts, Matthew. These young people are in need of hearing about Jesus—again and again and again. They don't need another parent or someone who is constantly 'watching' them."

Maybe he was right. I did put too much emphasis on all the wrong things they would do. In fact, just that night

I had taken those two young men aside and reprimanded them for using vulgar slang. I told them that if they continued using such language, they would not be welcome at youth group.

"I know, I know, you're right," I replied. "I need to learn to love the sinner and hate the sin. I . . ."

Dennis stopped me. "That's your problem," he said, pointing his index finger at me with excitement and exclamation. "Why don't you just concentrate on loving the sinner?"

Hmm. Just love the sinner, I thought. I had a million "buts" running through my head, but I remained quiet and let his words seep in. A feeling of embarrassment washed over me that night. I felt very humbled—too humbled to talk.

In the church today, we often spend too much time analyzing and judging the lifestyles of people rather than looking for a way to love them. What Dennis said to me made sense then—and it's a part of my lifestyle now. I was putting too much time and effort into seeking out the "sin" of those kids instead of looking for an opportunity to show them the unconditional love of Christ.

All of us need to lighten up with those who don't know Jesus. How can we expect people who are not Christian to act like or take on the characteristics of Christians? We can't enforce that. But we can seek out opportunities to love them. And the need for love is all around us. All we must do is ask Jesus to open our eyes and give us the ability to see humanity as he sees it.

However, asking God to open your eyes may be overwhelming at first. So beware. When humans begin to truly see the world around them with the eyes of Christ, the simple things in life look different. You'll find yourself aching over situations you once ignored. Your heart will reach out to those whom you would have once walked by. You'll begin to see people not as strangers, but as men and women who might need you to engage them. A simple elevator ride to the fourteenth floor becomes an opportunity to meet people and create relationships. Remember, you might be the only representation of Christ that person sees for the next twenty-four hours—learn to love him or her. Ask God for the ability to truly love people.

Christians talk a lot about love. It's so often the focus of ministries, sermons, and the like. Christian musicians sing songs about love. Who can forget the infamous song "They Will Know We Are Christians by Our Love"? (I believe that song must have been a prayer more than a statement.) Evangelists preach about love from the pulpit. Bible study groups study books on love. But despite being oversaturated with the topic, too often we are left with a very vague concept of what godly, faith-initiated love really is all about.

Love is a hard concept to learn (or relearn, as the case may be for some of us). But provocative faith requires us to reassess our human ability or inability to love one another and to love Jesus.

As I began to rethink my own affection toward God and humanity, Jesus showed me gaping holes in my life where love was absent. He showed me a picture of how inconsistent my love can be. He revealed places and instances where my preference to judge, ignore, or remain stagnant was crippling my capacity to feel or show love. There were times when I was tempted not to feel anything as I walked by a homeless man. Jesus stopped me in my tracks. He said to me, "I don't care what you think this man will do with the dollar you give him, he is my child, and I love him—that is all you need to know." Jesus was right. Every homeless man I ever walked by, I judged with thoughts such as *Get a job* or *He's nothing but a useless drug addict.* My heart for humanity was not "What can I do for you today?" It was more or less "How much can I get away with not caring about you today?"

Jesus zeroed in on the condition of my heart. He woke me up from a gross, dead sleep and demanded I (re)learn what it means to love. So many times, he had discovered me selfishly investing into a lifestyle that was meant to fulfill me. And I now realized how my misconceptions about pure, godly love had prevented me from living a life of love. My selfish, sin-filled heart was making it nearly impossible for me to show love toward the Father or toward others.

An individual's heart is the command center for a human's ability to show love. If one's heart is bruised, tainted, or unengaged, he will most always fail to show love. The Bible teaches that out of a man's heart comes what is good and what is evil. If our "command center" is not programmed or managed with the grace and mercy and justice of Christ, our ability to love is stifled, shut down, or nonexistent.

Personal trials also wreak havoc on the heart, making love a difficult action. So many of us have experienced painful circumstances in our lives that interfere with our desire to be reflecting Christ. When an individual has been abused, is battling depression, or is fighting anger, he is usually so consumed with himself that he can't show love. These circumstances certainly get in the way, but they are not excuses for us to be selfish lovers.

Jesus wants us to show love with complete abandonment. He taught this throughout his ministry here on earth. The catch is this: Jesus requests that this kind of love be shown toward God, family, friends, sinners, enemies, and even legalists. Jesus even got a bit sarcastic when he said that to love those who love you back is easy—even the worldly tax collectors do that. And he's right. Churches are filled to the brim with people who love lovable people. But if you want to know true love, if you want to capture the very heart of Jesus's teaching, if you want to tap into the extraordinary—love those who do not love you back or learn to love the seemingly unlovable.

Love is an outflow of what we feel on the inside. If our hearts and minds are set on the good things of Jesus, we will love, and we will love effortlessly. But too many of us are selfish. We think too much about judging, retaliation, and our own emotional stability. The bravest followers of Jesus are those who resist the urge to make everything about "me," and instead, turn that energy, emotion, and will toward loving others. *That's* what Jesus meant when he said to love your enemies. He wants us to respect them. He wants us to refrain from judging them. He wants us to stop fighting with them. *He* wants us to love them unconditionally.

In an earlier chapter, I told you that losing my job at *CCM Magazine* was a difficult experience. Well, when

I first heard the news, my instantaneous response was anger toward my new "enemy." (It's insane how quickly friends can become assumed enemies.) I wanted to retaliate. But Jesus said to be peaceful. I wanted to have vengeance. But Jesus said that he wanted me to love. I wanted to write a tell-all book about the company. Jesus said, "I want you to be quiet." I wanted the chance to reveal my version of the truth. But Jesus wanted his truth to be revealed.

Throughout my circumstance, Jesus began reminding me (and reminding me loudly) of what he wanted. I gave in and submitted to his will, and instead of turning my angst into revenge, I did my best to love those whom I thought had done me wrong. Loving those whom you feel have wronged you is a grueling task. That's mostly true because when you choose to love those who have hurt you or have become your enemies, you are relinquishing control. In other words, you are letting Jesus have his way. Your way, your understanding of the situation, gets put on the back burner. It's no longer the focus.

In 1996, my family and I were maliciously and unanimously voted out of a one-hundred-person small-town church in Maryland. The ousting happened because we had many disagreements with the pastor and his lifestyle. But in my opinion, the disagreements surely did not warrant excommunication. When we got the news that we had been voted out of a church, we were stunned, to say the least. People we considered to be good friends—our best friends—voted in favor of us being forced out of a house of worship that my mom and dad helped start.

Boy, was that a hard experience to endure. I could tear up thinking about the dismantled feelings my entire family battled. Simple trips to the grocery store, where we would pass our "friends" in the cereal aisle, would bring us home deflated and depressed. It felt like we had just had the wind knocked out of us. My sister and I once ran into the pastor of that church at the library. We wanted to cuss him out. I wanted to give him the finger behind his back. Oh, the anger toward him started in my toes and moved all the way up to the tip of my head. To love those people was an option, but at that time, it was one we were not ready to consider.

Over time, my family began praying for the ability to love. We prayed hard. But we just didn't (couldn't) feel it. They had hurt us. Our enemies had backstabbed us. Our wounds were still too fresh to even begin considering the concept of "loving" our enemies. But in time, Jesus invaded our situation and mercifully put us in our place. He gave us a glimpse of our hearts. He removed the junk from our eyes that refused to let us see what we had become. He gracefully showed us that if we truly desire to be like him, we will love like him, and that included loving those who had hurt us so deeply. I think one of my favorite attributes of Jesus is his passion to never let his children remain in the status quo. He constantly pushes us to move out of what feels comfortable and into the ugly, the desperate, and the fearful.

In circumstances such as these, humans who embrace the truth of Jesus often realize that in many cases we are relying on our own strength to love. We try to love. But we can't love on our own. True love can't be forced or pretended. It's lived. It took months of therapy, meditation, and hard conversations with Jesus before I was able to forgive the people in that church who hurt my family. I've learned the hard way that faith-driven love is a process one must submit to. It does not come naturally for us to love those who hurt us, adamantly disagree with us, or work against us. But Jesus says for us to love our enemies.

Provocative faith calls us to love relentlessly despite what we're feeling. Our personal feelings aren't calculated into God's equation of loving others. Unfortunately, our opinions and thoughts are not factored into the scheme of things. In other words, on the grand scale, Christians must love those who fight against Christian causes. It doesn't matter if individuals war in favor of abortion, other religions, sexual promiscuity, anti-Christian ideals, or more. Love is not conditional on opinions, issues, or politics. Jesus said to love our enemies. This means that we must make an effort to be kind and peaceful with those who rally against Christ. It doesn't mean we conform to or accept their beliefs, but it does mean we should love them. The battle to love those who rally against all that we hold dear is a difficult task—but one we must pray to understand and endure.

Gone must be the days of building our love around rules and litigations, policies and statements. Instead, we need to build our love entirely around the spirit of the living Jesus. It's his love living inside each of us that will allow us to love those who hate us and those who move to act against what we are passionate about.

Bigger and possibly more difficult to comprehend is our commandment to love those who have *personally* hurt us—backstabbed us, molested us, stole from us, said all kinds of untruths about us. It's those kinds of people who are *really* difficult to love. I'm talking about those "enemies" you have to see around your hometown, those you have to worship with every Sunday morning, or those you hope you never have to see again. When we embrace the truth that Jesus adamantly and offensively loves our enemies, only then will we ultimately be set free to love them too.

When we consider the truth that Jesus' sacrifice on the cross was a sacrifice for all of us—that his love is not manipulated or influenced by the conditions of humanity, belief systems, or sin—Christians can learn to love. I said in an earlier chapter that it's crucial that Christians keep going back again and again to the cross of Christ and identifying with the sacrifice. It's in this humble action that we see ourselves in relationship to Jesus and what he has accomplished in our lives. When we remember that it's only by his blood we are made lovable, then we will learn to love—and to love relentlessly.

Luke 6:35 says this: "Love your enemies! Do good to them! Lend to them! And don't be concerned that they might not repay. Then your reward from heaven will be very great, and you will truly be acting as children of the Most High, for he is kind to the unthankful and to those who are wicked" (NLT). I think I'll end this chapter with that. It says it all.

Man of God talks candidly about personal pain

Paul Canady was my pastor for five years. One of my most vivid memories of him is his tenderness toward people. His heart is bigger than he is—and he is a big man. Nearly every Sunday morning, the tangibility of the gospel of Christ moved Pastor Paul to tears. As one of my spiritual mentors, Pastor Paul with wisdom and compassion has often challenged me in my pursuit of the extraordinary. I interviewed him about his thoughts on painful circumstances and how he communicates the grace of God during such events.

MT: As a pastor, you have seen difficult times happen to a vast majority of people. What do you say to them when you first hear the news that tragedy has struck someone in your church family?

PC: At first, in most situations, it's not a time to say anything. It's simply a time to be there. Put your arm around them. Cry with them. Questions will come in the days ahead, and then you will have the opportunity to point to God's answers. But in those initial moments after the tragedy, it's important just to let them know you care.

MT: I know you, and I know you're an emotional guy; do you have to emotionally separate yourself from the situation to function as you think a pastor should?

PC: In one sense, I would answer this yes. If I am beside myself with emotion, then I'm not going to be of much help or strength to the other person. On the other hand, if I detach too much, I come across as one who does not care—one who doesn't have a handle on the gravity of the circumstances. I have always asked God to allow me to be wise in those situations and to have the capacity to comfort. At times, that means remaining very calm, especially if there is some hysteria with the other individual[s]. But nine times out of ten, "weeping with those who weep" is a very appropriate response. I almost always thank God for giving me a tender heart.

MT: I remember one tragedy in particular our church faced—the family's loss of a son in a car accident. Did you get angry at God during this situation?

PC: I do not recall getting angry at God, but I certainly asked him on a number of occasions, "Why?" I guess I have lived enough life by this point to have confidence in God's plan. I certainly have been surprised enough times by what he has produced out of storm clouds of life, to know that he knows what's best. My frustration comes in not always understanding God's choices. But still I trust his plan.

MT: During that time of trusting, did he speak? And if he did speak, was his explanation good enough, or did it take time for you to understand?

PC: I saw God do some amazing things out of that tragedy. Yes, I believe I got a glimpse of some of the answers to why. Several individuals responded to the gospel at that young man's funeral. A number of individuals renewed their relationship with God after hearing the testimony of how tender that little boy's heart was for his Lord. And it certainly made many of us a little more anxious to join Jesus in heaven some day. So, yes, I believe God gave me enough of a glimpse to trust that he knew what he was doing. My only hope is that I would be able to have the same response if it were my own son.

MT: Many times pastors are seen as the mouthpiece of God—laypeople expect pastors to have something really inspiring to say. How do you encourage your congregation to have an individual faith and not rely simply on the work of a pastor?

PC: I attempt to do this in a number of ways. One, I try to have a healthy transparency. I share my struggles, my questions, my inadequacies as a man, as a husband, as a father, etc. Secondly, I have never hesitated to remind folks from the pulpit that I am a fallible individual. Recently, I talked to my congregation about the Bereans in Acts who had the audacity to question the apostle Paul's teaching. And

Dr. Luke calls them "noble in character" because of it. I reminded the folks at my church that it is their responsibility to always check out what I preach, teach, or say with the Word of God. To never get into a mindset of thinking because Pastor Paul (or anyone else, for that matter) says it's true, it must be true.

MT: What event in the last few years has defined your own personal faith journey? Tell me about that journey.

PC: Okay, now you're prying! Just kidding. The event that most recently defined my personal faith journey was watching the church I had pastored for over fifteen years go through a split. Leading up to that painful experience had been a couple of years of excruciating discussion on the elder board behind closed doors. Finally, the unresolved disagreement among the leadership, primarily with one elder, broke out as a result of gossip and innuendo, as well as some unwise decisions on the part of the leadership. I was in shock at how quickly things fell apart from that point.

Certainly, most painful for me was the personal questioning of my character and integrity. Suddenly, rumors went wild regarding my personal life. Several stories about me committing adultery, stealing money from the church, covering up immorality among the church leadership, etc. had begun to flourish. I had never experienced such a painful thing in my life. It was the darkest period of my life. It was no doubt the closest I have ever come to leaving the ministry.

MT: Did your faith grow because of the journey?

PC: The "darkest period of my life" led to the greatest time of spiritual growth for me. I was driven to my knees. I had to decide whether or not I really trusted God in the midst of the chaos. I also was forced to reevaluate my ministry—reevaluate who I was as a pastor. God reminded me through this time that the pastor is a shepherd. He is to care for the flock. Love the people. Preach and teach the Word so that Christians mature in their faith.

MT: Most would probably say that "tapping into the extraordinary" is a process, a journey of sorts—how has God revealed the "extraordinary" to you?

PC: The times I have most sensed God doing the extraordinary are moments when I'm preaching the Word and it suddenly becomes very apparent that God is doing something in me or in the congregation that is way above my capability— words come out of my mouth that I didn't prepare; thoughts that I didn't have in advance; conclusions way beyond my wisdom. Then there have been times when I am totally convinced I have completely blown it. I am almost desperate to be done with the message so I can go crawl into a hole somewhere. And afterward, someone comes up and begins to tell me what God did in their heart through that message. I'm blown away because there is no doubt it was God doing something extraordinary. It's certainly not me.

9

engage faith-based community

In September 1999, a group of random acquaintances I met at a church invited me to join a Bible study that was geared toward "spiritually minded twentysomethings." It sounds cool, right? Well, to be honest, at that particular time in my life it did not sound at all exciting to me. When John, a clean-cut young man with an exuberant personality, approached me while I was enjoying a mocha latte at an Annapolis, Maryland, coffeehouse, I knew I was in trouble. John barely gave me a chance for small talk before he went right into his pitch with "Hey, Matthew, you want to join our Bible study?" At first, I did what every self-proclaimed abused Christian would have done—I panicked. John tried to make me more at ease by explaining, "A bunch of us get together on Tuesday nights, talk about Jesus, do some praying, and then we just chat for a while."

I just stared at him for a moment with a blank look on my face. With my memories from my past experiences within a Christian community bouncing through my mind, I could feel my heart beating faster at the thought of spending an hour in a small room with a homogenous group of over-engaged God-fearers. I honestly felt the urge to run to the bathroom for fear that I was going to be sick.

It had been almost a year since God had awakened me to my own personal spiritual revolution, but I didn't feel in any way physically or emotionally readied to share my experiences with others. Don't get me wrong; I was still going to church. I wasn't absolutely terrified of any contact with other "God-people." But I was carefully limiting my level of communication with church people—and I was especially anxious to avoid any kind of interactive situation where I would be expected to say something spiritual. Going to church as an almost invisible "pew warmer," silent and inactive, was safe; it ensured for the most part that I wouldn't get hurt. For now, I really wanted to keep my spiritual experience personal and firmly under my control. But as I sat there battling my overwhelming fear of actually talking with other Christians, John was watching me with that open smile and frankly inviting face. I finally gathered enough strength to tell him that I would think about visiting his Bible study. He grinned at me warmly and said, "Praise Jesus, I'll see you Tuesday night." I went home and vomited.

I showed up the first Tuesday night with considerable trepidation. I'm still not entirely sure why I showed up at all. Hundreds of thoughts were running through my mind: *Why am I here? I've been beaten and bruised by Christians too many times. Every time I find the strength to trust them again, I end up feeling like I'd rather be whipped than endure the unkindness and rejection of another group of "true Christians."* But the spirit of God was telling me to shut up, so I did—begrudgingly.

Entering the apartment, I noticed a faint scent of fake vanilla in the room. The aroma came from a few candles that lit the room with a warm, soft glow. Two girls, looking like young contemporary gypsies with their bandanas and spaghetti-strapped camisoles, welcomed me with hugs. A boy who looked like a recovering college jock offered to take my coat and scarf. His demeanor struck me as that of a feminized former naval officer. Either he was trying too hard to be humble, meek, and welcoming (just like Jesus), or he was the most mechanically nice guy I have ever met. I didn't know whether to shake his hand or get him out of there and beat him to a pulp.

It would be a major understatement to say that I did not want to be there. (Even apart from my fear of community, I wasn't too thrilled about missing NBC's Tuesday night lineup either.) But deep down, I knew I needed to stretch my spiritual boundaries and open myself up to the concept of being intimately involved in a Christian community once again. Yet I thought to myself, *Do I really have to experience that here?* It all seemed too formulaic for me. It seemed calculated—like the idea of community was being forced.

Community is an overused word in today's society. We're bombarded by it. Politicians talk about it, news agencies report on it, companies sell it, and churches preach it. In her book *It Takes a Village*, Hillary Rodham Clinton writes that it takes a well-established community to raise a healthy child. Throughout the nineties and into the new millennium, the television show *Friends* depicted most twenty-somethings' and thirtysomethings' idea of near-perfect community. The show about six beautiful individuals who loved each other, did everything together, lived close to each other, and laughed with one another became one of the most popular sitcoms of all time because it idealized the community that so many of us are missing. Secretly, all of us wanted to be a part of *Friends*. We desired to be sitting on that coffeehouse couch with Chandler and Joey, laughing with them, sharing in the wealth of joy and good times the cast depicted. Frankly, all of us want someone to "be there for us." We want to be surrounded by people we can count on no matter what.

And while mainstream culture sells, needs, watches, and reproduces community, churches claim to be community in its truest form. In his best-selling book *The Purpose Driven Life*, Rick Warren, pastor (and CEO) of Saddleback Church in California, emphasizes the importance of individuals seeking out Christian community for spiritual and emotional wellness. Some churches have built their entire existences around the concept of community. A friend of mine recently moved to Los Angeles to start a church ministry called "koinonia." The word in essence means community. But it certainly doesn't take someone with a degree in sociology to realize humanity has a deep need for the encouragement and stability found in our connection to other people.

All of us have heard the cliché that two is better than one. And for the most part, we believe it. I think it comes naturally for all of us to seek out friends who think as we do. We desire stimulating conversation with people we love because it is our hope that it will make us better and stronger individuals. When we're hurting, we want a shoulder to cry on. In times of pain, we need companions to walk with us through these difficult experiences. Christianity claims to be a place where these kinds of relationships breed. That's why most of us go to church—to worship with like-minded individuals. That's why we put a great deal of our energy into creating lasting relationships—because we need them.

And yet, as beneficial as it might be, community is difficult to enforce or create. I see Christians all of the time trying to create community with small groups, icebreakers, atmosphere, music, and the like. Some of these ventures are highly successful in terms of attendance and enjoyment, but it seems to me that they rarely reach true community; most break down into the shallow substitute of friendliness. Only on an odd occasion have I witnessed a church that was good at manufacturing community. Why? Because in most instances people cannot be forced or manipulated into experiencing community.

When I worked at the faith-based coffeehouse in Northern Virginia, our motto was "Music, Coffee, and Community." We set up plush leather sofas, served world-class coffee, and made sure the lighting was warm and inviting in hopes of making community more accessible. And there were certainly moments when I almost felt we achieved it, but those brief glimpses only made me realize how

143

difficult it really is to build true community. We want so badly to develop intimate relationships and to truly depend on each other; why is it such a hard thing to do in the real world?

The truth, as I realized when John invited me to that Bible study, is that many of us are afraid of community. We have locked ourselves away from becoming attached to anyone or anything for fear that we might get hurt. We have grown so accustomed to seeing Christians hurting each other and beating up on each other that we feel the need to protect our own emotional well-being by running from anything remotely close to community or any situation that might leave us vulnerable. And so our fear imprisons us. We give our hearts "to no one," as C. S. Lewis wrote; we take our hearts and "lock [them] up safe in the casket or coffin of [our] selfishness. But in that casket—safe, dark, motionless, airless—[they] will change. [They] will not be broken; [they] will become unbreakable, impenetrable, irredeemable" (*The Four Loves*, p. 121). Yet what choice do we have? We have to protect ourselves.

And yet, our obsession with the idea of community and relationship shows how much we need it. Jesus was certainly aware of our need for it. In fact, the word that the Gospel writers record as coming out of his mouth more often than any other—hundreds of times—is the word *with*. It's appropriate. If I had to sum the gospel up in one word, that might be it—the freedom to just be *with* God and be *with* other people. Paul describes the call of the gospel as "the ministry of reconciliation"—the job of getting people back together, with God and with each other. So I ask again: why is community so difficult?

I think that many times the church has gone about community in the wrong way. We love methods, and we love to think that the right icebreakers, the right discussion questions, or the right vanilla-scented atmosphere will give us the key we've been missing, unlocking our scarred and fearful hearts to the warmth of community. Unfortunately, it just isn't that simple. It takes time, and it takes courage, and it takes an incredible amount of risk. In a way, Christian community is a lot like marriage—it takes commitment and love and maybe even a little madness. You can't build real community in a six-week small group discussion or a ten-minute icebreaker. You can't get it by going around the circle and listening to everyone share three little-known facts about themselves. It takes risk, it takes time, and most of all, it takes life. Community is what happens not when you know that people *will* "be there for you," as it says in the *Friends* theme song, but after you've seen that they *are* there for you. It's through the experiences of life, and especially the difficult ones, that community is built.

While living in Northern Virginia, community took on a whole new meaning for me. Early on in my time there, I met Daniel Eagan. We became close friends almost immediately. Over prayer, good drink, and conversation, Daniel and I grew close. Over time, he introduced me to his friends. I introduced him to mine. Sooner or later we had a group of ten or so close-knit people who did all kinds of things together. We went to clubs together. We ran youth group programs together. We partied together. We cheered for each other. We worshiped Jesus together. We prayed together. It did not matter that many of us worshiped on Sunday mornings at different churches. It wasn't an issue that all of us worked different jobs Monday through Friday. Those differences didn't limit our ability to commune. We had Catholics in the group. We had Pentecostals in the group. And we had Presbyterians in the group. Even to this day, while many of us have moved away from the Northern Virginia area, all of us get together for weddings, birthday parties, and vacations. We talk on the phone. We express our needs to one another. I have no doubt that those ten or so people will be the ones who will strengthen me when I have to attend my father's funeral. They have been the ones who have challenged me when my life was broken from sin. And they will be the ones to celebrate with me when I am rejoicing.

While living in this reality, I realized I didn't need a church to define my community. I needed to find a small group of people who would love me not because it was part of the duty or simply part of the equation; I needed to meet people who over time would love me because it was a natural response to what they were feeling on the inside. To me, that's true community. Community takes time. It takes investment.

In his book *Waking the Dead*, John Eldridge describes Christian community:

> We hear each other's stories. We discover each other's glories. We learn to walk with God together. We pray for each other's healing. We cover each other's back. This small core fellowship is the essential ingredient for the Christian life. Jesus modeled it for us for a reason. Sure, he spoke to the masses. But he lived in a little platoon, a small fellowship of friends and allies. . . . Anytime an army goes to war or an expedition takes to the field, it breaks down into

little platoons and squads. And every chronicle of war or quest will tell you that the men and women who fought so bravely fought for each other. That's where the acts of heroism and sacrifice take place because that's where the devotion is. (pp. 191–92)

Provocative faith requires us to have this kind of group surrounding us. Community is not found in the nameless faces of the great army of God, spread out through history, but in the individual men and women you've fought side by side with, the people whose faces bear the scars they took when they defended you from the enemy, the people who've seen you limp and struggle and even fall and who pulled you back up out of the mud. Your platoon, your company, your friends; the people who pray for you and struggle with you and always watch your back. Ah, yes, that's community.

10

participate in God's dream for you

In July 2003, I was standing in front of a large group of people to talk about Jesus. The experience was strange, really—at least, it was for me. I'm not a world-class speaker; I'm not even sure I'm a speaker with any real class. I speak because I enjoy it and feel called to it, not because I am a naturally gifted communicator. But as strange as this situation felt, I think people actually enjoyed what I had to say. I mean, the people staring back at me were actually listening to my ramblings. They were giving me their undivided attention. People's heads were nodding at the correct times. They laughed and smiled when I said something funny. I heard a couple people shout in agreement when I said something they agreed with. For me, as a music business nobody with only a few professional conquests under my belt, the experience of talking about my faith in front of people was a bit surreal. However, it was not necessarily surprising.

After the event, when I was back in the comfort of my hotel room, I spent some time thanking God for the opportunity that he'd given me to talk about him. And that's when it hit me—I suddenly remembered that more than twelve years before, when I was a young kid still in high school, I had dreamed about this moment. I had dreamed many times—too many times to count—that I would be standing in front of large groups of people to talk about my faith and about God's mercy in my life. Going into this event, it hadn't occurred to me to see this experience as a "dream come true." But suddenly, when the event was over, it dawned on me that I had always known I was called to communicate faith. It was a childhood vision, a dream—something that was placed in my spiritual DNA by God for his glory. Can I explain it? Not really. But I believe in it wholeheartedly.

Now, before you begin jumping to conclusions, I don't want you to think I'm one of those kinds of people who get *lost* in the spiritual dream world. When I was a child, it was normally not my habit to get caught up in God-visions and dreams and stuff like that. I was raised in a very conservative church, remember? Anything remotely charismatic was deemed ridiculous by my church. So I was raised with a natural abhorrence for anything remotely spiritually dreamy or prophetic. After all, that kind of nonsense was said to be New Age spiritualism.

But even as I try to run away from anything remotely New Age, I have also experienced how God can use our dreams to advance his causes. Consider Scripture. God consistently used dreams to communicate his message to his people. Jacob dreamed. Joseph saw visions. Saul looked for God's answer through a dream. Daniel interpreted dreams. Joseph, the earthly husband of Mary, received the good news about the birth of Jesus through a dream. Still, while I knew these biblical stories to be true, I so often resisted the urge to believe that God would speak to me through a dream or a vision.

However, on that July day, when I realized that more than a decade before, God had given me the vision that I would be talking about him in front of many people, I couldn't help but be moved by God's powerful reminder that this dream (to communicate my faith in the greater culture) was given to me by him. This was his story being lived out in me—that although I had seemingly dreamed this would happen, it wasn't *my* dream; it was his.

Dreaming is a big part of how God interacts with his followers. I believe as Christians we are called to dream our wildest dreams, and then we are to submit to God's hand to fashion those dreams according to his will. We must learn to listen to what our passions are and what we dream of becoming. Those things are his heartbeat that he has placed in us. Each of us has God-dreams to dream. And only when we acknowledge his dreams do we really begin to live in the extraordinary. "In the Last Days," God says, "I will pour out my Spirit on every kind of people: Your sons will prophesy, also your daughters; Your young men will see visions, your old men dream dreams" (Acts 2:17).

At least a hundred times a day, I dream. I dream about how God desires to use me. I dream about my family's

151

future. I have dreams for my wife and me. I have selfish dreams about wanting my abs to look like Brad Pitt's and my biceps like Vin Diesel's. I dream about traveling around the world and investing my life into third-world countries. I still dream about what I'll be when I grow up (and I'm thirty-two). I dream about peace. I dream about what heaven will be like. I dream about seeing Jesus face-to-face for the first time. I never stop dreaming. I can't stop dreaming. Jesus won't let me stop dreaming.

All of us dream. Some of us have more active dream lives than others. I have been vividly dreaming since I was running around in diapers. Even when I was a child, the stories that jetted through my brain at night were action-packed, full-color minimovies with detailed stunts and graphics that no special effects designer could even come close to re-creating. The more information your mind has to play with, the more it has to work with to create a dream. And it's crazy how realistic dreams can feel. Your dreams can make you believe you're a superhero whose sole mission is to save United States intel from ending up in the hands of two Chinese drag queens who have a secret mission to bomb a large sports arena in Australia. (Yes, I dreamed that ridiculous scenario once.) Sometimes my dream life is so active that my ability to truly rest is interrupted. No doubt the dreams our minds create at night when we sleep can seem random, limitless, and bigger than life.

But I believe the dreams that God dreams for us are just as grandiose, ridiculous, and exciting. Okay, so he probably doesn't dream about us saving the world from

Chinese drag queens, but hopefully you get my point. God's dreams in you are an important part of your faith journey—not to be ignored, not to be forgotten, and never to be put aside.

Jesus is the author of our life's dreams. He probably doesn't care much about my dreams of having a Hollywood physique, but he wants us to dream. Jesus speaks to us through our dreams. He puts these thoughts and desires into our heart, and he expects us to follow through. Many times dreams define us—they're our calling, our reason for being, our passion.

I believe each of us has a God-calling on our lives that only we can accomplish. The Bible says that God knows his children, and that he knew us even while we were in our mothers' wombs. The word *know* here doesn't simply mean that God can put a name with a face. It's so much more than that. He knows us inside and out. He knows what will move us to tears. He knows what will make us jump up and down. He knows our talents, our fears, and the obstacles we'll face. And he knows our dreams. How can he know all of this? Because he created us—he created everything there is to know about us.

But the grace of God doesn't stop there. He gives us the ability to make decisions—good and bad. He gives us the freedom to listen or to ignore. He lets us choose whether we will face our fears or let our fears define us or limit us. And the same is true for our dreams. We can choose to follow our dreams, to chase after them with everything that we are. Or we can squash them, put them out, or set them aside. Jesus doesn't want us to set our dreams aside; he longs for them to be lived out and to bring him glory.

I met James Vans at a friend's Super Bowl party in January 2000. He was twenty-two at the time, a college graduate, and an extremely talented musician. He had always wanted to go into music and travel the world (or country or state or county) singing his songs. He told me that night that he had been dreaming of doing that since he was twelve years old. With that dream in his heart, he went to school to study music. He perfected his trade. And he even graduated with a couple of honors.

However, even though his degree was in music—acoustic guitar and vocals to be exact—James told me that he planned to find a local job in his hometown at a bookstore or coffeehouse "and just see what happens with my music."

James flew into Nashville last year for a wedding. He asked me if I would be willing to have dinner with him, and I said yes. Over vegetarian cuisine, we chatted at length. After a little chitchat, I started asking him some questions.

"The last time I talked to you, you were looking to work at a bookstore, right?" I asked, trying to figure out what he was doing with his life.

"Yeah, I'm actually still there, and I do some house painting on the side," he answered dispiritedly. "Life has handed me something of a bad hand lately."

"Well, at least you have a job," I said, trying to encourage him. "What's been rough about life?"

"Well, nothing huge. Just that good jobs have been hard to find, living with my parents has had its challenges, and I still haven't done anything with my music."

While listening to James, I couldn't help but be a little disappointed too. I tried not making it too obvious, but it definitely showed. "Dude, do you realize you said the same stuff to me the last time we chatted? And that was four years ago, bro. What are you doing? Where are you going? What happened to your music?"

James's face dropped when he looked up at me, and he said, "I had to stop dreaming, man."

"You had to stop dreaming?" I was astonished. Was this the same young man who had spoken with such passion of his lifelong dream only a few years before? "Are you telling me that you are no longer called to do music?" I asked him.

"No, not exactly."

"Well, what do you mean?" I demanded.

"I just got tired of the dead ends, Matthew." Exhaustion and disappointment were written all over his face. "I got tired of hearing people tell me no. I got tired of struggling financially. So I just let the dream die."

I hesitated. "I don't want to over spiritualize this, James," I said carefully, "but did Jesus let the dream die?"

For a moment, the passion I remembered blew across his face. Then it was gone again—snuffed out by disappointment. "I think about music every day of my life," he said impatiently. "Of course Jesus didn't let the dream die."

"Then I think you owe it to yourself to keep pursuing that dream."

Having worked in the Christian music industry for many years, I have come in contact with many good-hearted musicians whose God-dream is to sing. Because only a few select musicians are able to do Christian music professionally, too many would-be "artists" leave God's dreams behind because the record deal doesn't come through or a Nashville-based talent scout deems them "not good enough." Thankfully, God's dreams aren't contingent on what the world deems successful or profitable. I've met more than my share of extremely talented individuals whose God-dream was to do music. Unfortunately, too many of them quit after being told no. I've looked a few of them in the eyes and said, "Just because Nashville says you're not good enough to go on tour doesn't mean you have to let the dream die. Remember, this isn't your dream; it's God's."

All too often we are quick to let dreams die. We get tired of the hard work. We get frustrated because our dreams may seem to be different than when we were young. We let circumstance get in our way. In the Old Testament, Nehemiah dreamed of building a wall. He had obstacle after obstacle get in his way, but he would not let his dream die. Paul dreamed of reaching outside of the Jewish community with the gospel message. *Nothing* could come between him and his dream. Do you think Billy Graham stopped pursuing *his* dream? Do you think he had any idea that God would use him so extravagantly? He probably had some clue, but if he had given up, he would never have seen it come to pass. Consider my own dream of being one to communicate faith. Do you know how many people have told me that I am not good enough to be doing what

156

I know I am called to do? *Many!* And you know what? They're right. I'm not good enough to be doing what I have been given to do. But Jesus is. And the same is true for each of us. Sure you're going to feel as though you're in over your head. You're following Jesus! You will always feel you are in over your head. That's because in and of yourself you are not capable of fulfilling your God-dreams. But God cannot work a miracle in your life if you throw the dream away.

Theresa and her husband, T, walked into the Jammin' Java coffeehouse sometime in 1997. They looked at me and said, "We have a dream to start a faith-based coffeehouse and live-music venue out in Colorado." I smiled at them and gave them my best "That's awesome." But inside I'm rolling my eyes, thinking to myself, *Good luck. You know how many people walk into this store with that same dream?*

Theresa and T began asking me questions. They wanted to know the store's dimensions. They wanted to know how I booked the talent. They wanted to know what kind of coffee we served. They wanted to know every little thing about what we did at our coffeehouse. Theresa looked at me with a burning passion and said, "This is a dream I believe Jesus has given me to do. I know he has a purpose behind it."

All of us got around a table that night and prayed over the dream God had given Theresa to start a faith-based live-music venue in Colorado.

That was eight years ago. Theresa has since called me many times to give me updates about where they are with starting their coffeehouse. Some of the updates have been devastating. Some have been filled with joy. However, only last year did Theresa call to tell me that God's dream was finally becoming a reality—and that it looked much different than she would have ever expected. Are you actively participating in God's dream for you?

My dear friend Lisa Tedder always dreamed of working on a mission field in Africa. We'd stay up late talking about her desire to work among the poorest of the poor. Her eyes would sparkle at the mere thought of God using her talents in poverty-stricken Ethiopia. Lisa and I spent many nights praying over that dream—her vision, her heart's mission.

One of Lisa's most powerful gifts is working with teenagers. Very few people have the love, patience, devotion, and strength to put up with the burdened lives of troubled young women. But that was never a problem for Lisa. I watched God use her over and over again in the lives of hundreds of young women over a three-year period. Although youth ministry came easy for Lisa, the desire for the mission field still burned in her soul; it was a recurring dream that wouldn't let go.

One summer, Lisa was a youth leader on a mission trip to Romania. That trip changed her life. She came home and called me right away to say, "I'm moving to Romania."

"What!?! What happened to Ethiopia?" I exclaimed.

She just laughed and said to me, "Sometimes God's dreams change." Today, Lisa helps run a camp for Romanian youth in the poverty-stricken Jiu Valley in western Romania. Although she still holds out hope of one day going to Ethiopia, Lisa's heart was open to God's fashioning of her dream. She realized it was his story, not hers, that she was meant to live.

I learned something from Lisa. I learned that we must all be flexible to how God chooses to shape his dreams for us. God is not in the genie-in-a-bottle business. He doesn't say, "Make three wishes and I will instantly bring them to life for you." No, it's not like that at all. God expects us to push forward through this life with a passionate and persevering faith. When God gives us a dream, he doesn't promise an easy route to success or fame. On the contrary, it's his goal to make his dream for us perfect and stunning—like nothing we could have imagined on our own.

I meet too many people who are consumed with their own dreams and not the dreams God has planned. An individual pursuing provocative faith is not concerned with selfish dreams; he is concerned with the thoughts and plans that the God of the universe has laid out for each of us. Moreover, he actively pursues the dreams that God has instilled in him. All people, Christians and non-Christians, dream. The difference is that for Christians, the dreams must ultimately result in glorification of Jesus and serve his purpose, not ours. If you have a dream of becoming a celebrity just because you think it would be awesome to walk the red carpet and see your name in lights, chances are that may not be the dream God has for you. But if you dream about being a celebrity so you will have opportunities to share what God has done in your life, then not only continue to dream, but begin to actively pursue that profession.

Do you see my point? It isn't so much the dream it-self, as it is the action of making it a reality to give God the glory he desires and deserves. If God has given you a dream, and chances are he has, it is imperative that you seek his will on how to make it a reality. Never lose focus on the truth that the dream is a blessing and a gift from Jesus. But in the end, don't you want to hear, "Well done, good and faithful servant"? I want to hear Jesus say to me, "Matthew, you took my dream in you and made it what I wanted it to be; good job!" I believe that pursuing your God-given dreams will play into why some glorious day we will hear those words of affirmation. After all, weren't those words originally addressed in the story to the servants who pursued every opportunity to increase their master's riches and grow what he had given them? God has given each of us a little portion of his treasure—a dream that is the passion of our hearts, a dream that matches perfectly with our gifts and talents, a dream that only we can achieve. What we do with it is our choice. We can bury it in the ground and let it die. Or, we can be provocative and risk it, spend it, invest it, gamble it, and daringly pursue it to its fulfillment in our lives and in the kingdom.

11

be an individual; rely on Jesus

In its fall 2004 ad campaign, Gap Inc. asked, "How do *you* wear it?" In support of its new campaign slogan, Gap ran magazine ads that showed sexy models dressed in layered Gap clothing. Each ad purposefully encouraged original expression in the way that we dress. The how-do-you-wear-it question reeked of a challenge for Gap patrons to be individuals, to stand alone with a personal fashion statement. Gap Inc. created a special website for its campaign, and a bus painted with Gap's logo toured the country and gave away free style consultations. But in the end, were people really dressed all that uniquely? Was this truly a campaign about individuality?

I don't think so. Ultimately, those who fell for Gap's adage ended up wearing the same sweater as Sarah Jessica Parker, Gap's paid-for star power. Sure, some of us put a collared shirt underneath our blue Gap sweater, some of us wore the sweater under a jacket, and some of us wore it tied around our waists, but in essence, it was the same sweater—all of us who wore the sweater made pretty much the same statement: "Hey look, we shop at the Gap."

It doesn't take a nuclear physicist to see that the clothes we wear say very little about whether we possess "individuality" or not. Nevertheless, the battle cry of individuality sparks big business in today's culture. So many businesses, from fashion companies to soda manufacturers, are selling their products by using some type of individuality message. We are constantly being bombarded with messages that boast about the need to "just be you." Product ads encourage us to stand up for our beliefs. They remind us that it's okay, in fact, it's welcomed to be loud and proud of who we are and what we love. Marketers believe that if they can convince us that their product will help us individualize ourselves, we will buy what they are selling. In today's media-drenched culture, being an individual (someone who is independent, unique, thinks on his or her own, and isn't swayed by popular opinion) is a cumbersome task. Advertisements and marketing ploys don't make the conquest to be an individual easier; they complicate it.

All of us at one time or another have been led astray by a company's savvy marketing schemes in hopes that "having it, drinking it, wearing it, or doing it" would make us feel cool, relevant, and original. And for small amounts of time, such things really do make us feel alive. I mean, when my mom bought me my very first Coca-Cola T-shirt in 1987, I thought I was the coolest "individual" around. But unfortunately, the particular "it" we fancy usually becomes a trend, and *usually* in the end, the "it" we so desperately needed to feel alive loses its cool factor because everyone has, drinks, wears, or does "it."

I can't tell you how many times I've gotten lost in pursuing "it" for individuality. In college, I went through a very "dark" stage. I dyed my hair black—no big deal, right? But it didn't stop there. I wore huge, black combat boots with crazy-colored socks that were pulled up to my knees. This look might have been fine if I hadn't been wearing funky cutoff denim shorts. To complete the look, I wore a ruffled, white tuxedo shirt underneath a retro, seventies-style blue blazer. *And yes, I thought I was cool.* I had a friend tell me once that I looked like an ex-clown on heroin. But quite honestly, I welcomed the attention (good and bad); I thought my clothes made me an individual because they made me stand out in a crowd and people watched me wherever I walked. I loved that. I craved the "individual" attention my fashion statement—or lack thereof—allowed me.

It wasn't too long before I gave up my sad, dark fashion statement and moved right into wearing loud, brightly colored club shirts. Everywhere I went, I made sure I was wearing a shirt that made people talk. I had a shirt that looked like aluminum foil. I had a couple shirts that literally made people sick or dizzy to look at. My poor mother almost disowned me over those ridiculous shirts. But I didn't care because I was intent on being what I thought was an individual. Now, over the years I've come to realize that there's nothing wrong with looking like a clown on heroin, but when you rely on your threads to define your individuality, you have a serious problem.

I don't care who creates "it" or says "it" is the cool thing to do. "It" doesn't satisfy our human desire to be original and relevant. Sure, society says otherwise. But Jesus, in all his glorified wisdom, breaks down this thought process.

Nicodemus, the guy well-known for the question about being born again from his mother's womb (John 3), thought too that what he did and wore and followed made him an individual. His questioning produced one of my favorite conversations between Jesus and a potential believer. It's a dialogue that speaks blatantly about what makes humanity truly relevant. Jesus told Nicodemus that he could not even begin to see the kingdom of heaven unless he was born again. Jesus's words refute what so many still believe will make them individuals of significance.

There was a man of the Pharisee sect, Nicodemus, a prominent leader among the Jews. Late one night he visited Jesus and said, "Rabbi, we all know you're a teacher straight from God. No one could do all the God-pointing, God-revealing acts you do if God weren't in on it."

Jesus said, "You're absolutely right. Take it from me: Unless a person is born from above, it's not possible to see what I'm pointing to—to God's kingdom."

"How can anyone," said Nicodemus, "be born who has already been born and grown up? You can't re-enter your mother's womb and be born again. What are you saying with this 'born-from-above' talk?"

Jesus said, "You're not listening. Let me say it again. Unless a person submits to this original creation—the 'wind hovering over the water' creation, the invisible moving the visible, a baptism into a new life—it's not possible to enter God's kingdom. When you look at a baby, it's just that: a body you can look at and touch. But the person who takes shape within is formed by something you can't see and touch—the Spirit—and becomes a living spirit."

John 3:1–6

Despite Jesus being crystal clear about what makes us each relevant people, Christians continue to be handicapped by the lack of individualism in their faith. No, it's not the media hampering our ability to be individuals as people of faith; more often it's our churches setting the rules and mandating what makes people relevant and original in "Christian" culture as well as the culture at large. I believe that now more than ever, we live in a time when it is imperative that our churches not *define* our relationship with Jesus and not *alter* the way Jesus has designed each of us to be—individuals defined by a strong love and understanding of our Savior.

For more than twenty years, my faith was molded and defined by a church. While I was in that particular church (for fifteen years), I was like a sick man on life support. Instead of being a healthy, breathing, life-filled follower of Jesus, I relied on a church consumed with rules, bad theology, and its own terms to do what it knew how to do to keep me breathing. Unfortunately, that church's methods didn't work. The "machine" certainly worked to keep my heart beating, but I couldn't move without assistance; I couldn't get up and walk across the room without someone holding my hand. I was spiritually handicapped. I was living by someone else's idea of "being Christian" and not God's idea. During this time, technically I was alive. But I was far off the course from *truly* living. The idea of church—following its rules, its way of worship, its methods—consumed me so much that it began to steal away the simple joys, graces, and mercies that a person of individual faith is supposed to grasp. Instead of helping sustain me, the church made me feel crippled.

Jesus never intended for his followers to be crippled. It was never his goal to bring bondage upon people, especially within a community of believers. On the contrary, his message was about freeing us from what we held onto, freeing us from the sin that consumed us. While he walked this earth, he came to *heal* those who were sick, crippled, and lifeless. And he still makes that his priority today.

Scripture teaches us that the church was designed to encourage people of faith; it was meant to be a community of like-minded people devoted to loving and being like Jesus. I don't believe the politics and theology of church were ever meant to define our faith. Church was never meant to be the life force on which we put our strength, hope, peace, and confidence. And it can't be that place. *Individual* relationship with Christ is where those things are. Yet in today's Christian culture, the *mass* production of modern Christianity has often made church a form of life support for believers rather than the community of believers it's meant to be. But it doesn't work. Instead of our life in Christ being supported, church often puts us on spiritual crutches that steal away our ability to be free, to be individuals.

Okay, so I know I am walking on fragile ground with this chapter. You could take what I have said as direct criticism of the church and its theology. But that is not my goal. Basic theology built securely on biblical principles is of utmost importance to our faith. And involvement within a community of believers is a powerful tool that Jesus uses to strengthen and encourage and evangelize. However, I also know that our pursuance of individuality in our love and faith for Jesus is essential to us truly being able to tap into the spiritually extraordinary. And when a particular church's study of God or its politics or its pastor or its belief systems take precedence over our individual exploration and experience of Jesus, God's work in us to complete us is more often than not hindered.

The church should be a catalyst for Christians that inspires and encourages us to focus on Jesus. It should point us toward a more compelling and grace-filled relationship with him. A church should be a place where followers of Jesus can be individuals and pursue the dreams, goals, and visions God has given them.

People who pursue provocative faith must not let the church define their relationships with Jesus. If your church adds anything to the gospel message, you're on life support. If your church dictates how you should worship, you're on life support. If your church is led by pastors and teachers who are out for their own glory, you're on life support. If your church lacks direction, a mission, or a clear vision for community, you're on life support. If your church is consumed with having the biggest building, creating a theme park, or boasting of its campus, you could very well be on life support.

Eight years ago, I realized I was surviving spiritually by living on the life support of a church. Once my eyes were opened, I made a promise to God that I would never let anything other than him define my relationship with Jesus.

I don't believe very many of us wake up in the morning and say to ourselves, "I want to be just like everybody else. What can I do today to conform?" In fact, I believe most of us desire a little more out of life than simply conformity. I think it's only natural for humans to have a desire to pursue a spirit of individuality. And especially when it comes to our faith, I believe Jesus enjoys the differences that each of us brings to our relationship with him. But so often out of fear and lack of faith, I think many of us have a tendency to cling to what feels comfortable and safe, and we resist what is outrageous, daring, and provocative.

And although that kind of fear is a natural part of the human experience, to give in to that fear is paralyzing. Moses didn't lead the children of Israel out of Egypt by being fearful. Even though early on in his life Moses was codependent and lacked confidence, God made him an individual who eventually relied fully on his power. When Esther first learned what she had to do to save her people, she was scared. But God took an ordinary woman and did extraordinary things in her life because she was willing to be an individual. Jesus was often exasperated with Peter. But despite Peter's unbelief in the early stages of his faith, God made him an individual who ultimately spoke at Pentecost and witnessed the miracle of three thousand people coming to know faith in Jesus. Despite their fears, foolishness, and unbelief, God took ordinary people and made them individuals reliant upon provocative faith in Jesus.

Provocative faith sometimes requires us to stand alone. God uses these instances as times of growth in the life of his followers. We aren't truly living unless he is pushing us outside of our comfort zones. That's why we're here—to help live out his kingdom here on earth. If we remain where it is safe and comfortable, we don't truly experience Jesus. Every man or woman of God in Scripture faced situations or circumstances where they had to be individuals, where they had to stand alone on the promise that God would not leave them nor forsake them. Every one of us has God-responsibilities we must surrender to. Being an individual is not about what you wear or drink or have, but it is about what you do and who you are. And if we let Jesus take our humanity—all our mistakes and stupidity and talents—he'll take "it" and make "it" something worthy of changing the world.

12

your life isn't yours

Let me tell you why you are here. You're here to be salt-seasoning that brings out the God-flavors of this earth. If you lose your saltiness, how will people taste godliness? You've lost your usefulness and will end up in the garbage.

Matthew 5:13

As a kid growing up in Chapel Hill, North Carolina, Gerald Sims had always told his father that he wanted to be a lawyer, just like Dad. Sims came darn close to fulfilling that dream. He graduated with honors from an Ivy League college. He was accepted into one of the most prestigious law schools in the country. But about six months into his law school experience, Sims ran smack into Jesus on the way to class one morning.

"I could not get away from this feeling that he wanted my undivided attention," said Sims. "I *really* tried to keep walking the long walk across campus from the parking lot to the law building, but he wouldn't let me be. He kept saying, 'Sit down; I need to talk to you.' Finally, after failing to ignore him, I said out loud, 'What do you want?'"

Sims laughed out loud recalling the experience.

"People started staring at me, wondering what in the world had gotten into me. I think they believed I had gone insane. And maybe I had gone insane. But I didn't care. I sat down on a bench nearby. And this is what I heard him say: 'I want you to go to Moscow and be a missionary. I've already prepared the way for you to go. All you have to do is obey.'"

Surprisingly, Sims never questioned what Jesus said to him. He immediately decided to skip his class and drive right over to his father's office building. As soon as he walked into his dad's corner digs, his father looked at him and said, "You're here to tell me that you're dropping out of law school, aren't you, son?"

"What? How did you know that?" asked Sims in utter shock.

"I just had a feeling; I've been praying for you all morning," said his father nonchalantly.

"And you're okay with this? You're not mad?"

"No, I'm fine with it. You need to go do what you gotta do. Who am I to stand in the way of God using you?"

Roughly six months later, Sims left his career, his job, his BMW, and his family, and boarded a plane to Russia. Today, he lives on the outskirts of Moscow and works full-time as a missionary at a Christian relief organization. When Jesus called his name, Gerald was there, ready to listen and obey.

Stories like Gerald's happen all the time. Jesus is known for his interruptions in life. He gets away with things like that. Jesus is constantly calling his followers to leave all they know and love and follow him. Ever since Jesus called his first disciple, people have been giving up their lives in pursuit of following the causes of Christ. We've all read the stories. We've heard the testimonies. We've even cheered those people on! Gerald's story is simply one of a million stories of Jesus asking humans to give him everything. There have been CEOs of multimillion-dollar companies who have become missionaries in third-world countries. I've met doctors who have left their $150,000-a-year jobs to work in foreign medical clinics where they barely get by with enough medical supplies. I get goose bumps hearing such stories; I am amazed by such great faith.

But isn't this exactly what provocative faith in Jesus requires of us—that we give our lives away for "who knows what" in return? I'm sure Gerald would have loved to hear Jesus say, "If you follow me on this one, I'm going to give you [fill in the blank] as a reward." That would have no doubt made the decision easier. That would have at least given Sims something to look forward to. But Jesus doesn't usually give us an explanation as to why he is calling us—he just calls us and expects us to follow.

I cannot help but get excited every time I reread the story of Peter walking on water. Call me crazy, but it excites me to see people run headlong into what Jesus has for them. Peter had such a fanatical faith that it was practically impossible for him *not* to jump out of the boat and pursue Jesus. It was second nature for him to at least try. Peter had a faithful abandonment that was probably partly just immaturity and mostly pure desire. It's almost as if he didn't know any better. He followed what his heart was telling him to do. His eyes were fixated on what he knew he wanted in life—to know Jesus fully and to follow him with everything he had. In fact, Peter anticipated the chance to join Jesus out on the water. He asked Jesus if it was possible. So, without question, when Jesus called Peter to join him on the water, Peter jumped.

Would you have jumped out of the boat? Or maybe I should ask this: *Do* you jump out of the boat? Do you anticipate the chance to jump out of the boat and walk with Jesus on the water? Does your faith require you to forget about all that you fear, forget about the waves that are crashing all around you, forget about the job you can't stand, forget about the nice things you've gathered along the way, forget about the health problem that keeps you pain-stricken? When Jesus calls your name, do you jump at the chance to meet him wherever that might be—even if he is in the midst of the waves, walking on water?

I truly believe that most Christians *want* to be where Peter was that day. We desire to be walking on the water with Jesus. We want to be so enamored with Jesus that we leave everything behind and pursue only him. Unfortunately, too many of us stay in the boat. We fear that we might fail. We fear that we might have to leave behind our possessions. Our fear cripples our ability to give our lives away completely.

Today's culture (like many cultures throughout history) is consumed with wealth, fame, external beauty, and personal gain. If you can dream it, you can have it, keep it, store it, invest it, grow it, and get more of it. And it's not just people like Oprah and Bill Gates who suffer with such problems; all of us have to fight against our human nature to be consumed with selfish gain. You don't have to look too hard to find people who are consumed with fulfilling only their selfish dreams. Even among Christians, the war against being overcome with the need for possessions wages hard.

As we know, followers of Jesus are called to be different from the rest of society when it comes to our need and lust for possessions. We're called to have pure and selfless priorities. We're called to put no stock in the *things* of this world. We live in a time when it is much more difficult to give ourselves away because we now have so much more to lose. But Jesus says lose it. He says not to store up "junk" here on earth. Matthew 6:19–21 says, "Don't store up treasures here on earth, where they can be eaten by moths and get rusty, and where thieves break in and steal. Store your treasures in heaven, where they will never become moth-eaten or rusty and where they will be safe from thieves. Wherever your treasure is, there your heart and thoughts will also be" (NLT).

Do we believe this to be true? Do we honestly believe what Jesus said in these verses to be true—that creating treasures here on earth is a waste of time? I know we quote these verses a great deal, but do we believe them? I meet so many Christians who are completely consumed with materialism and power—so much that their ability to give their lives away is handicapped. Jesus knows what possessions can do in the life of someone who follows him. That's why he talked about it being harder for the rich to enter into the kingdom, because he knows how our possessions can hold us back from truly abandoning our lives and pursuing our Father.

On January 1, 2002, six of my good friends and I woke up at 5:30 a.m. to help feed the homeless as part of a Washington DC project. The shelter was just like any other you might find in cities around the world. While there, I spent my time making pancakes, rolling hot dogs into buns, and ladling green beans and instant mashed potatoes onto the plates of the nearly two hundred patrons who frequented Miriam's Kitchen.

By 9:30 a.m., we were back in the comfort of our posh living conditions—complete with heat, a cozy bed, and an eight-person hot tub. But before my friends and I ventured home, we stopped and ate breakfast at Bob Evans. We spent that hour or so talking about the New Year's Eve party we had enjoyed the night before with eighty-five of our closest friends, where there was lots of music, a midnight prayer gathering, and the camaraderie of many great relationships. In other words, compared to the homeless men and women we had just served with so-so food, we had it made.

To be honest, I felt really good about myself that morning. *Hello?* I had just gotten up early on New Year's Day and spent three hours with people who were less fortunate than I was. *Why shouldn't I feel good about myself?* I dashed my "salt" and shined my "light" with the best of them that morning. You would have thought I had just fulfilled some kind of God-quota. And in my mind, I guess I had.

But maturity and spiritual understanding have reawakened me to knowing that engaging the world with the love of Christ requires much more than simply getting up early once in a blue moon and feeding the homeless. That's certainly a good start. But in all truthfulness, giving ourselves away requires a change in lifestyle, a change in the way we think about the world around us, and a change in the way we understand the nature of Jesus.

Many of us tend to look at culture from the outside. For most of my life, I viewed the greater culture as something I observed—something I watched from afar. I flirted with getting involved. I spent $28 a month to sponsor a starving child. I fed the homeless every six months or so. I went on a few mission trips. I taught a kids' Bible study. But my actions weren't growing out of a heart and mind striving passionately to engage culture with a kingdom perspective.

Janet Smyth, a twenty-nine-year-old social worker, left her familiar surroundings of Little Rock, Arkansas, in 2002 and went to work for a children's adoption agency in Peru. She told me via email last year that her main reason for going to Peru was personal conviction.

"I'd been asking God for a long time to give me some life direction," wrote Janet. "It felt as though I wasn't getting any answers, until one day I was reading Jesus's request to Peter to 'feed my sheep.' I was like, 'Bingo! That's what I am supposed to do.'"

Today, Janet makes about $185 a week helping abandoned children find permanent Christian homes all around the world. Janet gets what it means to engage culture with a kingdom perspective. She realizes that her life is not hers. I believe it is the call of Christ that all of us get to a place in our spiritual walk where we resist the temptation to just be comfortable; I believe we are called to look for opportunities to give our lives away for potentially *nothing* in return.

But we can't all move to the Third World, can we? Is Jesus out of his mind? No, but he does have some pretty big standards for us to live up to.

Engaging the world around us begins with the condition of our hearts. Just as our hearts determine whether we relearn how to love, whether we are content being last instead of first, and whether we live a lifestyle of joy, likewise our hearts navigate how our minds, hands, feet, and words will serve the communities around us. If we have conditioned our hearts to only serve the almighty "ME," that's exactly what we will do. We will be selfish. Why? Because that is what our hearts are trained to do. We will follow wherever and whatever our hearts treasure. Just like Matthew 6:21 says, where our treasure is, there will our hearts be also. The Bible teaches that our hearts will follow whatever we cherish, put first, and hold sacred.

You show me a person who is truly advancing the kingdom of God through his or her deeds, and I guarantee that individual has a heart fixated on knowing Jesus and helping people. We humans can learn to push our hearts out of the comfortable and away from what is normal into a life and a mindset of serving and engaging others. We just need to be willing to do it. We need to be willing to lose ourselves in the process.

Engagement in the world has everything to do with pursuing Jesus with reckless abandonment. It is not the money we give to charities or the random volunteer service activities we participate in (I would call that limited world engagement). Rather, it is doing everything and giving everything to show Jesus to the world. In its simplest terms, the world includes everyone who does and does not know Jesus. Engaging the world does not mean only engaging a segment of the population. It means engaging everyone in whatever ways you can to show that you actually care about what's going on in the lives of people. Do your next-door neighbors know you care about them? Does your boss have any clue that you are very much concerned for his or her well-being? Do you know the name of your Starbucks barista and actually let him or her know that you're not just another customer? It's in these kinds of circumstances that we begin to engage the world. And while *many* people are called to go all around the world and serve communities abroad, *all* of us have people in our neighborhoods who need to be engaged with the life of the gospel by someone provocative, someone willing to take a chance.

For many of us, it's a simple issue of time. We are surrounded by needs; we are surrounded by people who are hurting, who are lonely, who are hungry, who simply need an open ear. But so many times we walk by them, not even noticing. We are blind to the simplest things around us. I believe that engaging the world means neither more nor less than simply opening up our eyes and our hearts to the things that are going on in the people around us—not just on the surface, but in their hearts—and not just the people in our community, but whomever we find ourselves faced with, no matter where God calls us, anywhere in the world.

One night a few years ago, I met a friend at Friday's for dinner. Actually, we were having an informal business meeting; we were discussing an article that my friend was writing for me for *CCM Magazine*. Under normal circumstances, I would have been completely focused on the business at hand, but we were both quickly distracted from our discussion by the poor service of our waiter. I've had many interesting experiences at restaurants, but I think I can say without equivocation that this waiter was absolutely the worst I have ever had in my entire life. After half an hour of sitting in the restaurant, we still hadn't even ordered our drinks. I could feel my irritation level rising, and when he finally did come to take our drink order, it was all I could do to speak civilly while asking for an iced tea. A few minutes later, however, I went to the men's room, and in my moment alone in the stall, God spoke to me. (Yes, God talks to me in the bathroom!) "Matthew," he said, "I want you to talk to this waiter about me."

At that point I wasn't sure I was even going to be able to talk to the waiter about my dinner order, but at least the awareness that God was doing something that night changed my perspective. Suddenly I found myself observing the evening from the waiter's point of view. I watched him as he hurried around the room from one table to another, and I noticed the worry and distraction etched on his face. And gradually, I began to feel compassion toward him instead of irritation. And when he next (finally) came to our table, I found myself wanting to talk about him instead of about me and my needs. "What's your name?" I asked him. "How long have you worked here? Is it a busy night?"

"Oh, man," he breathed, "yeah, it's a rough night."

Even with my God-induced empathy for the guy, I'm sure I was still less friendly than I usually am to strangers. But I guess God must have been working in his heart too, because the next time he came by our table, he said unexpectedly, "You guys are really cool. Can I come talk with you next time I have a minute?"

I don't usually get such friendliness from waiters, but at that moment I knew that something powerful was going on. "Of course," I said, and a few minutes later we were three sitting around the table. And before we knew it, our waiter was sharing his heart with us—how he'd known for years that he was infertile because of a sickness, but the previous day his girlfriend had told him she was pregnant with his baby. She wanted to have an abortion, but he really wanted the baby—particularly since he knew, even though he didn't believe in God, that that baby was a miracle. My friend and I talked with him, shared with him, and prayed with him. I don't know what happened with his situation, but I do know that we were the divinely designated "God-incarnation" for that moment in his life.

God might never call you to travel halfway around the world or to live among the poorest of the poor, but there is no doubt in my mind that he is calling you to be his incarnation. Every day, every minute, everywhere you go, there are needs all around you, and the call on your life is to open your heart to them. The call is to open your eyes and your hands, to be willing to take the time. It takes time to listen, time to open your heart to someone else's needs. You have to reprogram your mind to an awareness of the truth that God is working all around you, and that he wants to work *through* you as well.

That's what Jesus wants from us. He wants us to open up and be willing to talk to the person in the elevator, in the grocery store, or at the gym. He didn't move halfway around the world to share the love of his Father with the people around him; he did it right there among the people of his community. And if we are truly living a life outside of ourselves, then it becomes natural for us to respond to the needs of people in our circle of influence, our communities, our country, and our world. This is our calling and our invitation. The challenge for us is to live it.

conclusion

be provocative

I tell you the truth, if you have faith as small as a mustard
seed, you can say to this mountain, "Move from here to
there" and it will move. Nothing will be impossible for
you.

Matthew 17:20 NIV

Let's suppose that Jesus decided to come and give the
Sermon on the Mount during the early years of the twenty-
first century. Imagine for a moment that you are on the
mountain the day when Jesus speaks the words of his
famous sermon recorded in Matthew 5–7. You're there
with a group of friends. Think of yourself as simply one of
thousands, maybe millions, in a crowd hearing this would-
be Messiah speak words, thoughts, and opinions you have
never heard before. Consider the impact this God-man's
authority would have on your heart as his words scrape
against all that you believe or have heard before. His words

offend you; they offend your politics, your morality, and your religion.

Imagine what your reaction would be when you hear Jesus say out loud for the first time that you are supposed to love your enemies, turn the other cheek when someone punches you in the face, and be a peacemaker when you desire to fight back. Your heart and mind would no doubt be filled up with some kind of emotion, some kind of movement. Perhaps you're quite angered because his words contradict what your pastor or priest said the Sunday morning before. Or maybe you're surprised, shocked, and bewildered that he is so honest and upfront about the human condition. You might think he should mind his own business and go back to where he came from. His teaching might have mesmerized you. Or it might have simply moved you to cry. No matter what you're feeling or thinking at the time, you walk away knowing this man, this God, is someone you want to know, someone you want to hear more about. His message intrigues you.

If your response is anything like mine, you're probably getting a small taste of what you felt when you heard the gospel of Jesus Christ for the first time. Remember your curiosity? Remember how it upset you? Remember the excitement that welled up inside you when you first felt the Spirit move you? You could hardly contain yourself, right?

The first time I remember being moved to respond to the message of Jesus, I was a child. I sat in the pew with this eager and electrified nervousness running through my body. The need for repentance and redemption ran heavy through my veins. I didn't understand it, but it was there.

I responded. I responded with tears. I responded with excitement. Although I certainly didn't comprehend the power that I was introduced to that day, I do remember leaving that moment changed.

Over the years, my heart for Jesus has swayed a bit. Parts of my journey have been poorly chosen pathways and shortcuts. And there have been moments when I've climbed staircases when I should have been enjoying slides. But through it all, I've felt the power of Jesus as he walked alongside me as my guide on this journey. I've heard him speak. I've felt his disciplining hand against my backside. I've sat in his lap. And I've run from him. In other words, I've lived life.

Through it all, one thing has not changed: my faith is provocative. Many of my friends questioned why I chose to use the word *provocative* in a book about faith. I use this word because I know that if the life of a Christian reflects anything close to what Jesus intends, the result is provocative, controversial, stimulating, and confrontational. When a follower of Jesus loves his enemy, the world listens. When a follower of Jesus decidedly makes a choice to be last, communities watch in awe. When a follower of Jesus works as a peacemaker instead of creating more problems and more walls, the office is suddenly shocked. Why do all these things happen? Because when we respond the way Jesus asks us to, our actions grate against the norm. Suddenly, the kingdom that Jesus spoke so passionately about is happening in front of you. And if that's not power, I don't know what is.

Jesus gave us a guideline in his words for kingdom living. Now, the world scoffs at such wisdom. And even churches often make light of Jesus's more provocative statements. But the fact is that either what Jesus said when he was here on earth is completely true, or we are wasting our time. The apostle Paul said as much in his letter to the Corinthians, when the church was questioning some of its more extravagant and controversial beliefs. If that's the case, Paul said in essence, if the challenging, extreme, and controversial truths of Jesus's words are not truths, then "we are to be pitied more than all men" (1 Cor. 15:19 NIV). If these words are not true, Paul said, then our lives are worthless and pitiful, because these words, these truths, have formed the foundation of our lives and our ministry.

What about you? Where would you be if the truth of Jesus's claims and guidelines were taken away from you? I believe that too many of us would still have a foundation to stand on, because we've built our foundations on something else. On the comfort of our family, on knowing the right words to say or the right face to wear, on getting a good job and collecting material things, or on finding good friendships and relationships to enjoy. All of those things can be good, and many of them can be a comfortable base for your life. But none of them will lead you to a powerful and provocative faith. And none of them will lead you into the purpose that God made you for.

Yes, it is frightening, and yes, it is a risk to truly build your life on the words of Jesus and on a relationship with him. But that is the only foundation that will take you walking on the water and make the waves into a place as safe and secure as solid ground. It is the only foundation that will make you into a person who is provocative, who is always challenging those around you to grow and to become more real. It is the only foundation that will make you into the whole and authentic person you were truly meant to be.

So start now. Come out of your cage, and let go of your fear. Listen. Watch. Empathize. Be real. Be provocative. Be free.

afterword

I would have rather done almost anything than read another book on faith. Faith is supposed to be one of the core tenets of our belief system, and if you don't get it after hearing the words of Jesus, studying the Bible, and listening to kumbaya-Christian radio, you might need to see a doctor. So you can imagine how excited I was when Matthew sent me his new book and asked me to read it over.

Fortunately, I decided to read the first chapter. And then the second. And then the third. And then the rest of the book. When I finished the last page, I remembered something about my good buddy Matthew. He gets it. He doesn't water down the truth with a bunch of simple anecdotes, and he doesn't tiptoe around the controversial issues that affect this generation. With humor and wit, he reminds us that we are not called to simply believe the Scripture and verse but the one whom the Scripture and verse reveals.

I've read most of the stuff Matthew has written, and I've even had the opportunity to sit down and have coffee with him a couple of times. It doesn't matter the topic—politics, religion, music—Matthew speaks with a maturity well beyond his years. Sometimes I agree with him, and sometimes I don't. But I'm *always* impressed with his red-hot, unfettered, unbridled passion. His faith is hotter than car seats in summer and twice as sticky. So, if anybody should write a book about provocative faith, it should be a man who walks on the water with the Savior and calls the rest of us out of the boat. I couldn't have done it. But I'm honored that he has allowed us to take this extraordinary journey with him.

Provocative Faith calls us to cultivate a transforming and Savior-like faith. Furthermore, it speaks to the necessity of unhitching the past's problems, unlocking the cage you have been imprisoned in, unraveling the web of deceit around you, and running, weeping, and wailing into the Father's arms. Like me, as you read, you probably couldn't help but become infected with a faith that takes you from where you are to where you are destined to be.

I guess the best compliment that I can pay Matthew is this: Of all the Christian writers trying to fearlessly share the truth, he is one of the few that I don't want to pound into ashtray sand.

And that's too bad. I think I could take him.

Jason B. Illian
motivational speaker and author

Matthew Paul Turner is a social and cultural commentator for today. The author of *The Christian Culture Survival Guide* and *The Coffeehouse Gospel,* he has also served as editor-in-chief for *CCM,* the nation's leading Christian entertainment magazine, and music and entertainment editor for Crosswalk.com, the world's largest Christian website. Matthew is also a frequent contributor to *Relevant* magazine. He and his wife, Jessica, live in Nashville, Tennessee. For more information, visit his website at www.matthewpaulturner.com.

World Vision

"Right now, World Vision is helping save the lives of millions of children. Whether a country is hit with famine, or by AIDS or natural disaster, World Vision is there reaching out to individuals and communities with things like physical, emotional and spiritual help. I'm asking you to sponsor a child and help World Vision continue to be the hands and feet of Jesus throughout the world."

- Matthew Paul Turner

Worship God
by sponsoring a Child!